This book is dedicated to Mum and Dad,
Shami and Tariq Khan,
For being there.

Cover Designer - Ares Jun

N.A. Khan (signature)

My Journey

A condition that forever changed my life

A True Story

N.A. Khan

Dedication

To mum and Dad who inspired me to always work hard and try my best. None of my successes would have been possible without my parents. Encouraging me to go on every adventure, especially this one. Listening to me and offering any assistance or help when writing this book. Through hospital, it must have been tough watching, waiting, and staying by my side day in and day out as I continued to get worse day by day. Minute by minute deteriorating. But yet again, I couldn't have gone through it myself. Though I was adamant, it was you two who tried and tried, again and again to make me accept my condition and the many disabilities in which, I have. But, many times, I would say - shouting at me wouldn't make me accept it. And that's when you would realise that I should be told not shouted at. For, believing in me. A can do attitude where everyone else assumes I must lack in everything - good for nothing! I submit my heartiest gratitude to Dad. For taking me to my lengthily hospital appointments and ensuring I maintain my motivation in attending them all. I remember at one point, I was like, cancel them all, there's no point. It's not as if I have a cure. The never ending medical appointments and the many A&E and ambulance visits we were to endure, during the course of the night. The long-ass wait. Suffer and tolerate! Making sure my educational-life flowed smoothly. Though I hid my disability and didn't wanted to be seen as any different, it was you who ensured that all the right services were put in place - guaranteed to make life easy for me! The number of meetings and ensuring I have all the necessary help regarding my needs. Giving me the opportunity to experience and to enhance being behind the wheel and to undergo many driving lessons. A great experience!

Whereas, I extend many thanks to Mum. Running around like a headless chicken, providing food on the table for the entire family. Making sure we are clothed, washed and fed. It was you who tried to build up my confidence and tried not to make me so paranoid within the family though I failed greatly. There was realistically no point, how can you fix a low confidence, nervous wreck? You can't! Reading this, will give you the answers you've always wanted, why I keep myself to myself, why I think these things, and what made me like this. A paranoid mess, seemingly. You may express your emotions in many ways in that you may cry and feel what I feel when you read about my daily struggle, my feelings or reading about the hospital times. People may even think that I'm a self-centred, egocentric and self-obsessed. Feeling sorry for myself, exhibitionist, extravagant, and, a self-centred freak with my so called sob stories as they don't usually like hearing the truth regarding, my feelings as they may even shut off to any emotion. But this isn't dedicated to anyone but my parents, who have been through literally every up and down with me. So I am positive it will touch you somehow to a certain extent. But consecutively, you will admire my determination and the vigour and power never to give up and carry on. First when I thought about getting my story out, I thought to myself, *nah… no one will want to know, let alone read it.* But then, one day, a thought sprung to my mind. *Actually, people may feel my pain, they may learn something from this.* That's when it struck me. To materialise my biography and since that day, I just kept writing and writing. Putting my thoughts together. And I never know? It may touch someone, somewhere, somehow – Well, I hope so.

Many thanks
To you both!
xxx

Acknowledgements

First, I'd like to thank the wonderful D.G Torrens, the inspiring author of such an outstanding and comprehensive biography, *Amelia's Story*. She is passionate, motivated, and dedicated in what she does. Thank you for talking me through the publishing process and offering me reassurance for proceeding with such a big step!

Of course, thanks goes out to the lovely, Aunt Zara, for giving me the great opportunity to meet the great, D.G. Torrens. I wouldn't have known where to start if it wasn't for you. I just knew my intent would have been fulfilled since the day you introduced me to D.G. Torrens!

I want to express my gratitude to many of my loved ones for being a part of my life, starting with, Faye Dixon, my A-Level tutor. Without you, I wouldn't have had the confidence in believing in myself. There were so many times when you comforted me when I was feeling down; you gave me the courage to think positive, putting aside any negative thoughts. A positive inspiration to me while, I was a student of yours.

I revere the patronage and moral support extended with love. My Parents, whose financial support and passionate encouragement made it possible for me to complete this project. For giving me the strength I have each day. Thank you for sharing your knowledge on various aspects of life with me, for providing me with clothing, food, and shelter over my head. And thank you for being willing to listen to my ongoing questions - quite annoying as they are! Thanks are also due to my brother and sisters in this regard.

I would also like to thank, Francis Titchen, (the "nice" Scottish lady) my learning support coordinator, for providing me with one-to-one help whenever I needed it and referring me to the relevant agencies that would meet my needs. Though it was a nightmare encouraging me to go to counselling sessions, the fear of knowing they may discuss me with other agencies was overwhelming, nevertheless, you always extended a hand.

I would like to thank each and every one of you at Wilson Stuart. I would not be the person I am today! Furthermore, I would like to take this opportunity to thank the West Midlands Rehabilitation Centre. Orthotic's Team, (Oak Tree Lane), for their on going support, helping me with my walking. I am so grateful to the doctors for saving my life. Without the specialists who have been involved within my care: Dr Geoff Debelle, Children's Paediatrician at the Children's Hospital, Birmingham; my Neurologists who have been continuing with my adult care ever since; the late Dr. S. H Green, Consultant Paediatric Neurologist, also at the Children's Hospital. The college psychologists for protecting me against a statement of Special Educational Needs.

I wish to thank the people who constantly put me down, telling me to quit with education. They have only given me the strength, determination, and the drive never to give up!

Embarking and Embracing on what's in front of me and brushing off any Negativity.

I am so fortunate to have the wonderful English team at Matthew Boulton; they inspired me with such positive and persuasive feedback on elaborating and continuing with the original version of my Biography. Enabling me to research on such a hot topic. It was due to your positive response while being a student at your college. It was you who motivated me to go into writing.

My friends, thank you for showing me freedom and for being there whenever I needed someone to listen to. I would turn to you and you would give me your 100%!

And finally, I extend deep gratitude to all my readers out there. It is you that I write for. After all, it is you, my followers who give me the confidence to know that I will be a successful author, even during the process of getting my manuscript ready.

Prologue

This diary was written on November 7th 2013. It had always been my intent to write and to eventually publish my manuscript. Back at school, it had always been a dream that I could never fulfil. However, now it seems that someday I may be able to accomplish, (my long-awaited dream.) My objective is to publicise this book once I graduate. If for any reason I'm not around, I would give this honour to my Dad or in his absence to my sister, Zara Khan.

This extended biography started out as a short story that I wrote in 2010 for one of my GCSE English Language classes. Inspired by others and their approving feedback, I decided to write my autobiography. In general terms, this book gives an insight into my experiences and the difficulties I forever encounter. How I have adapted throughout the years, coming from a special-need background and going into a mainstream education. For those featured in the book who wish to remain anonymous, initials have been assigned at random to ensure privacy of information.

"Being a great source of comfort and support, I hope I will be able to confide everything to you, my

diary. I have never been able to confide or express my thoughts to anyone, therefore I am pleased to dedicate and rely on this book as my voice. "Anne Frank

My story discusses the ways in which people have ignored my disability as an excuse to fuss over me, my negativity towards my condition, and my wish to be accepted in society. For many years, I hid my disability, brushing it under the carpet as if it doesn't exist. But later on, I did realise, I was only causing more stress to myself. Despite my difficulties, which I forever encounter, I now vow never to let my disability get me down. No more crying myself to sleep. I can proudly say I have achieved quite a lot despite still wishing for that miracle, when one day I would wake up to find myself completely normal—no difficulties, no fuss, not being a burden on others. Will my wishes ever be answered?

Having read many books on people with disabilities and specific difficulties, I realised their stories are not so different from mine—the way people see you (stereotyping,) the many things people take for granted, and the things that we *disabled* sacrifice. *Clarity, The Fault In Our Stars,* and s*he Is Not Invisible* have all been amazing to read, but my favourite was, Sharon M. Draper's incredible and captivating, *Out Of My Mind: "Being diagnosed with a disability,11-*

year-old Melody has a photographic memory. Her mind is like a video camera that is always recording constantly. Is there a delete button? She's the most intelligent kid in her whole school, but no one knows it. If only she could speak up, if only she could tell people what she thinks and knows, but how can she, because Melody can't talk. She can't walk. She can't write..."

This outstanding and touching book takes me right back to when I was flat on my back, not being able to walk or talk. One particular element that stood out from the rest is when doctors and loved ones gave up hope. It evoked a memory of being back in hospital when my family was told I may never speak, walk, and even move ever again. Not being able to do anything. But obviously, I proved them wrong. Therefore, each limb that I managed to move brought celebration. Even when I scratched my nose it was noteworthy.

A majority of people in my family dislike me. Most likely because, I'm the straightforward, truthful, plain, and upfront one. People act as if nothing's wrong. As if ignoring me is completely normal. You know that feeling when you can just sense it? As they lay their eyes on me, but, a moment later, they look away as if I wasn't there. But how can you deny yourself when it's all written in black and white? People intentionally disregard and overlook me. It's as simple as that. They act as if I'm not there. Sitting in total silence. Refusing to take notice of my presence when I'm directly sat in the same room opposite them. I feel the fact that people know it gets to me, is more than enough. But, rubbing it in even more to wind me up is just evil and deceitful. And for that reason only, I avoid people. The awkwardness and cumbersome of it all, is just frigging too much for me as the uncomfortable and deadly silence lay on my skin like poison as it seeps into my blood and paralyses my brain, pupils becoming dilated. The sound of clattering as mum washes her dishes in the kitchen. *I can't just get up and leave the room because I'll just end up falling,* so I pretend to look down at my phone and that I can't exactly do for the whole day. *Why is it only me* I wonder? *It's not as if I have DISABLED, printed on my forehead.* I try not to let it get to me and just play along and sometimes avoiding people is the best policy there is. They may resent the fact that I live at dads - but who knows? *People only respect you one you have a good job and the people like me are seen as a no one.*

The way I see it is, if you don't like someone, you shouldn't pretend to like them. But then one day, Dad taught me the world doesn't work like that. It is one big game. People will pretend to like one another despite burning up inside with either hate or jealousy.

Because, jealousy is popular in my family. Everyone has a bad opinion about someone but yet, to their faces, they're all lovey dovey. Complimenting and praising them.

I got there in the end... eventually "People treat you dumb. Use that to your advantage." Too many people nowadays, they think it's a competition It's nice to be nice. Complimenting others. Praising and admiring. Charming, pleasurable and yet so gracious.

But no, instead, people do the total opposite, in an attempt to make themselves look clever by throwing sarcastic insults and comments by mocking and teasing. Saying the opposite to what they mean in an attempt to make someone else feel stupid. Annoying the people who can't get their jokes. Deliberately going too far to offend the person.

Being brutally honest can sometimes get me into so much trouble. I don't like it when people pretend to like one another, impressing and making others happy. What is the point when they can see right through one another? But, it's hard being a blunt person in a family where people lie and bitch about one another... Being honest and straight up isn't accepted in society yet. Putting on an act to please and impress someone is fine - I don't get that.

It did take me quite a while to realise that I can't and won't be seen as a *normal* person in society.

Sometimes I think to myself that people are so narrow-minded that they don't acknowledge me as an individual, but as the disability in itself. The offensive comments people make, the mimicking and the way people's perception towards disabled people. The way they regard it, understand my weaknesses, struggles, and the barriers in which I had to break to move forward have all been understood and interpreted the wrong way. People make judgments and assumptions on the word, *disability.* There is more to me than my condition, but no, people generally perceive the disabled as lacking in literally everything. Okay, putting aside the verbal comments. It's just the small little things, like the gestures make me want to say, *"I'm not dumb you know. I do understand."* Perhaps I was better off being knocked up as a dead useless vegetable. That way, I wouldn't know the difference between good and bad and right from wrong.

Diagnosed with a chronic illness is kind of shit, really. The constant hospital appointments telling me I'm slowly and gradually getting worse, contaminating more and more each day, waiting when everything would be taken away from me as I weaken, wear away, decompose, and fade. Doctors only see me on a regular basis, keeping an eye on me and not doing the most valuable and important thing. Well, according to me, that is. I did ask my neurologist if they could maybe perform an operation so I could walk better and straighter. But, he just said, "no, there's a high risk, it may not even work." I was heartbroken but I presume, that's because, my balance has nothing to do with my legs but with the brain in itself.

The day I was left broken and constantly living in guilt. Not being able to do what I could and what I should and the many sacrifices in which, I had to make for a step to move on. I had always been so negative about my condition. I have opened up a little to a certain extent since learning from my learning support coordinator. Francis Titchen. Francis had been a great help, but yet again, she understood that after such a traumatic event. I found it intensively difficult to accept. Accepting my weaknesses and complex needs. Balance and co-ordination rapidly and gradually vanish. The awkwardness of it all putting a lot of stress on me. Faced with many challenges and health conditions—Arrogant. A nuisance. I mean, I can't even write. Do you know how bloody annoying that is? Great, my coordination is gone—what next? The times it really hits me- is when I can't even read myself.

Being young and sick, is sort of like being elderly, except we lack the reflection on all the great times and great things we did long ago. Instead, we watch our peers make the memories and strides they'll look back on fondly, bitterly observing and praying for our chance, our time! For many of my years, I hid my disability. Brushing it under the carpet, as if, it didn't exist. For most of my college life actually. I would hide the fact that I have something wrong with me. What lies behind me and what lies before me, are tiny matters compared to what really lies within me. Risking using the stairs, avoiding lifts. Risking myself tumbling down the stairs in the event of a fire, where dad got involved with the principle and then contacted learning support to put procedures into place and the necessary support. They said, I was too *head strong* and not wanting any help, but at the end, I had to own up. Probably the fault did lie within me. Wanting to be treated and seen as any normal person, not wanting them to recognise my weaknesses - the areas in which, I fall. And the alarm and fear of people discussing me, judging me. And providing so much help that you can just see that I'm an abnormal person.

Four years, I successfully, efficiently and positively went around without them having a clue about my needs. Being treated as any other normal student. I would sit my childcare and IT exams and would pass them with flying colours. My writing was way better then, until 2011 onwards! The time my condition started deteriorating. The worsening of it. Regardless of whether I liked it or not, I was given support. Someone to take me from one classroom to the other. I was to use the disabled lifts no matter what. Taking in what had happened in the past. When I would deny the fact that I needed any kind of support, risking the stairs and, seeing the disabled lifts as an embarrassment. Not wanting college tutors and lectures to be aware of my needs despite, knowing that all this, would put a lot of, anxiety, pressure, tension and, a great amount of worry on me. As I was, reluctant to open up to others. I was now provided with extra time and a scribe in every exam. A person I would dictate all my answers to, which I hate. My writing was no longer comprehensible. Processing of information had slowed down and my walking and co-ordination had rapidly and increasingly worsened. Hiding my embarrassments and the forever sacrifices that have become a part of my life. Overcoming many of my obstacles, but the eternal battle that lives within me will probably never fix.

The darker moments in life are the ones us humans should respect and value the most, most life lessons are learnt through darker moments in life_ Hussain Mesnani.

Synopsis

Born at: Dudley RD Hospital, Birmingham
Birth Date: 19th February
Status: born a Normal kid
Weight: 9 Pounds
Hospital Name: Hannah

Back when I was a child, there was never a time when I was *perfect*. I was always an uncoordinated and clumsy kid and there was no doubt about that. It stopped being funny the time I was found flat on my back, a victim of my tragic illness.

I was brain dead at the age of seven—diagnosed with a *disability*. There's that word I hate. Labelling me with a word that is so abnormal.

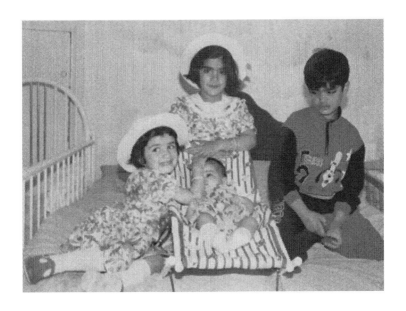

The image above with myself and my siblings: From left is me, my eldest sister, Sanam, my brother, Tamour, and in the middle, my youngest sister, Zara. There are four of us in total. I was the only one not to graduate. Tamour, graduated from the University of Birmingham after doing a degree in Civil Engineering. He then did his masters. He is now a qualified GCSE Mathematics teacher after a year of doing a PGCE at Keel University. 2015, he got married to, Dr. Muneeba Ahmed and continues with his teaching at Jordan for a year.

Sanam, my eldest sister, graduated from Leicester University with a qualification in Medicine in 2010. She had a commitment of five years of training and had the great opportunity to shadow my consultant and paediatrician, Dr. Geoff Debelle at the Children's Hospital. She put her work and skills into practice, which involved various aspects of medicine. She is now working at Heartlands Hospital with a three-year training program of becoming a qualified GP in her chosen area of work. In 2016, she passed her final exam and is now a qualified GP.

My dream at an early age was to become an optometrist, but apparently I need to be sensible about my options. Misguided and on the wrong course, I'm currently working around that... well, trying to.

Zara, my youngest sister, graduated in 2014 at Aston University, Birmingham. She studied Chemical Engineering and has recently completed her Master's in pharmaceutical engineering. Receiving a free scholarship for her final year as well as an internship in China.

The dark horse of the family. Since many had no expectations of her, but yet, she proved everyone wrong. Coming a long way from school, being too laid back about her studies, constantly getting shouted at. To the present day, where she has achieved more than a degree! She has now been offered a job in Hull, (Yorkshire.)

MY STORY IS BASED ON MY EXPERIENCES AND CONSISTS OF REAL LIFE EVENTS

Summer 1997, I was diagnosed with encephalitis, which is the inflammation of the brain and is said to be triggered by a severe viral infection. Up until now, neurologists and paediatricians could not pinpoint the cause of my illness, leaving me with unresolved questions. I remember at the age of seven, my whole world shattered. My speech was impaired, I had no control over my movements, and my co-ordination was lost. I was broken. In my mind, I was a new-born again— lying in a room where I could not talk, I could not walk. What is normal? Normal was throwing a tantrum, but what was there to understand of just a mumble? I had no choice but to come to terms with it all and to understand that this is the new me, whether I like it or not.

My name is Nadia Khan and this is my story…

Chapter 1,

Early Days

Before I was even diagnosed, I was an extremely clumsy child, coming home with grazed knees each and every day. I often fell so violently that the school playground would actually shake and vibrate, leaving my tights painfully stuck to my knees as the blood would literally pour out where my tights had been pulled loose.

Even holding onto someone's hand, I would collapse to the floor. But, why though? There was no reason to fall. There was no uneven ground or objects to be aware of. No, I was a clumsy child and that was that. I even used to fall from a sitting down position and to be honest, I still do because of my weird balance. Who falls from a sitting down position? I sway from side to side and then I'm on the floor.

There were also occasional incidents where I would spill the homemade curry of what mum had made. The list of tumbles, tripping, and hurting myself was endless. Getting shouted at was normal. I had expected it. I had a routine of getting shouted at each time I would fall.

To any other parent, it would be quiet obvious that this could be a symptom of something, as normal kids—or should I say, "abled children"—would not just collapse on such occasions without reason. But it did not occur to my parents at the time.

Early Signs and Symptoms:

We were on break for the summer holidays when it all changed. It was a weekend. I was in the garden playing on the swings and slides with my sisters and cousins when all of a sudden, I came down with the flu, suffering from severe dizzy spells and bad headaches. I could no longer make sense of where I was going; it was all just a blur, going around in circles.

Finally, making my way inside with great difficulty, I started complaining that my head was banging. Swaying uncontrollably and not being able to keep still, Dad took me to the living room and noticed my speech was slurred and no longer comprehensible. He took me to the doctor, our GP, with signs of expected flu and was prescribed with Paracetamol.

A week later, when dad was at work, we had guests over. Being in bed, my cousin, Nayyar Zaid, was feeding me a plate of rice. Mum called me from the bottom of the stairs, "Nadia, auntie has come. Come and meet her."

As I stood at the top of the stairs, I swayed from side to side and nearly toppled down, but luckily Mum quickly grabbed hold of me. I was confused and unaware of what was going on around me. Mum immediately paid another visit to the GP's and yet again, by Monday instead of improving, I was actually getting worse. The doctor again prescribed me with medication and sent me back home. Probably not any wiser. How could he possibly have known there was something seriously wrong with me? After all, I was just showing flu-like symptoms and it was only later on that I was getting worse.

Not receiving the right amount of attention and care, Mum decided to take me to the A&E department. By this time, I couldn't walk, couldn't see, was constantly sick, and suffering from an extremely bad headache-like migraine. I was immensely lethargic.

Mum immediately called an ambulance to take Mum and me to the Birmingham Children's Hospital where dad had followed... taking an early leave from work.

I was in the exam room with the specialists when I blacked out. A number of nurses and doctors were all involved in my care and were carrying out all sorts of examinations to get to the bottom of what was happening to me. Instantly, I was put on a drip due to a severe form of dehydration and it wasn't till a few weeks later, I was diagnosed with a rare disease. Shortly after my collapse, my family had gone home, since it was after visiting hours, and they too received the heart breaking phone call.

My parents were demanding an answer, someone to say that I was going to be all right. However, the doctors could only say they were doing all they could and would let us know of any update as soon as possible. My parents had no choice but to wait for hours. By the time the consultant was able to update them, it was already past midnight. He sat them both down and said, "*We have been monitoring your daughter, but we do not as yet know the cause of what has triggered this off. So, may we reassure you, your daughter is in safe hands. We are doing our best to find out what is going on and once we do, we will let you know as soon as possible."*

My parents were desperate for a diagnosis, but they focused on hope. That day, I was admitted and mum was to stay with me over night. By now, the extended family had been notified of the news, but they too had to wait in the comfort of their own homes.

A few days later, in the early hours of the morning, Mum had to update Dad on the news. Ringing him at work, she said, *"The doctor would like to speak to both of us regarding Nadia at about 12 noon."* Rushing to the hospital as early as he could. They would have been so nervous sitting in the waiting area, but remained calm for my sake as well as their own. The Neurologist arrived and said,

"I am pleased to meet you Mr. and Mrs. Khan. I am Nadia's neurologist, Dr Green. I understand that Nadia has experienced some dizzy spells and bad headaches. Can you please elaborate on this?" Dad gave a brief outline and a summary of the incidents that led up to my admittance.

Dr Green, then took a moment to absorb all the details and asked some questions regarding the points discussed and then continued, *"We have been doing all sorts of tests on your daughter and as a diagnosis, we have found that it is a rare illness called, Encephalitis. Encephalitis is the inflammation and swelling of the brain. This is usually caused by a viral infection or the body's immune system, mistakenly attacking brain tissue and has many impacts and on-going issues. Generally, encephalitis begins with a fever and a headache and the symptoms may worsen. There may be incidents of confusion, drowsiness and loss of conscience, which I understand that you have already witnessed. As we are aware that each individual reacts differently, this may lead to a coma, but please, may I reassure you, we may not even come to that stage. It is our duty to inform families of the worst-case scenario regardless of whether it happens or not."*

Mum and Dad did not understand. It was all happening so fast. Every day of being kept in hospital would involve more and more tests. On some occasions, they would repeat the tests, but they did not think for a second, of all the pain and grief they would put me through.

Initially, I was in the high dependency ward and then transferred into the Intensive Care Unit for a couple of days. Doctors tried many medications, trying to improve my symptoms. However, they did not know what the exact cause was.

Many weeks later, I woke up. I had speech challenges. I had a hard time speaking and couldn't connect with people as easily as before. I had to relearn everyday tasks from scratch—walking, talking, moving, and eating—the basic skills that we all take for granted.

I had to endure numerous lumber punctures, x-rays, and MRIs, (brain scans).This meant going into a long, endlessly noisy tunnel in which I had to lie completely still while they took images of my brain. Both sides of the tunnel were securely locked, making me feel intensely claustrophobic. I couldn't move; it was too tight in there. The loud engine noise drowning out my screams. I could feel a warm shiver of fright all over my body. My cries were not listened to, I was ignored. *"Keep still, keep still!"* They would say.

Being in intensive care was rather scary. I could hear my heart monitor racing, *beep....beep....beep... beep,* with every two seconds of Mum being frightened to death. On receiving the distressing, and sad news, Dad really did find it intensely agonizing, torturous, and grievous, seeing me like that as I constantly and vigorously, fought for my life in a way that involved gathering all my inner and physical strength. Holding onto each moment as if my life depended on it. As my eyes slowly and gradually open and close in slow motion. I still remember the nurse saying the exact words to Mum, *"your daughter hasn't got long to live."* Mum's cry howled through the entire room! Sometimes I regret surviving that moment, where I could have shared my last breath, but then again who doesn't have bad days?

Another test involved sticking wires to my head. This monitored my brain activity and its brain waves through its circular probes. These probes in red, green, and yellow were stuck on the end of each wire and attached all over my head. This particular test was quite painful and had usually ended with me pulling off the wires. These wires were attached to a computer monitor, which had monitored my brain pattern. Nurses and Doctors would reattach these wires to my head to get a clear reading.

The nerve conduction test was another painful examination. This test consisted of attaching red, blue and green wires to me, examining my touch senses and nerve pattern. I had to sit completely still. This was impossible for me to do as my back muscles were weak, I was unable to sit unsupervised. So, I was held upright in a chair while doctors had twinged each wire, making every bit of my body jump in pain.

I was now put in ward 9, with the rest of the kids. I did not have my privacy except the grey curtain I had just outside my room to draw around me if ever I wanted to be alone, shutting myself away from the other children.

A monster trapped inside
a new-born's body

Having lost my appetite, I was now fed through a drip, a long and narrow tube that went down my throat. When this tube trickled out of my nose from mum trying to lift me from one chair to the other, the tube would get stuck in the side of the chair and pull out my nose piercing. Knowing what was coming next, I would scream and shout. Eyes wide, mouth rigid and open, face gaunt and immobile. My fists clenched with branched knuckles and nails digging deeply into the palms of my hands.

The alarm would strike. Nurses would charge in rapidly as though an invitation was off limits. They were there to push the tube back up my nose. Making a terrible snorting sound, I could feel an irritating sting as though the tube was being pushed up my throat and a shooting prickle down my nose. It would go up my nose and down my oesophagus. Two of the nurses would hold me down, one to keep my mouth open wide enough and the other, to stick the wire down my throat, literally choking myself to death.

Primary school friends and teachers all visited me. Not being able to talk or express my feelings hurt so badly. It was as if I was a statue in bed. The only thing I could do was scream and shout. Knowing that no one understood me made me want to throw my arms and kick my legs, as though I was having an epileptic fit. So irritating.

Family would visit often, on a regular basis. They were all gathered around me, talking amongst each other as if I didn't exist. Well what choice did they have? It wasn't as if I would casualty sit up in bed. (Eyes flashed open, gasping for air.)People would sit on the edge of my bed. Kicking my legs, I would tell them to scoot.

Useless, Pathetic, Pointless.

Day by day, I was transformed into a beast. Eating away at my hands. If Mum couldn't make sense of what I was trying to say, which was complete gibberish, then I would explode with resentment and eat at hers too. I was a vicious aggressive ogre. I was now given mittens from the nurses to stop me from chewing at my hands. Mum was told to sleep separately from me and no longer in the same bed. I feel for mum for putting up with that. Even though, she was no longer in the same bed as me, I would imagine, she would constantly have the fear of me waking up, screaming and shouting in the middle of the night and most likely having sleepless nights.

Joshua was my neighbour and was five years old at the time, two years younger than me. He had given me a Tamagotchi cyber-pet, a dinosaur. It needed feeding, potty training, exercise, and putting to sleep at the right specific times. Whenever I was asleep, my sisters would take it home to look after it for me. I used to throw such a fit once I knew it was gone.

Dr Green, my brain specialist, would pay me daily visits. He would carry out all sorts of examinations. He must have been a top brain consultant as he had students on placement shadowing him. He looked like Albert Einstein with his grey hair. Dr Green and his students would surround me, forming a narrow circle. On these visits, I would end up in tears, frightened at the people around me. I was then referred to Dr Geoff Debelle, children's paediatrician and consultant. Dr Debelle was such a lovely man and so understanding. He would pay regular ward rounds, usually every morning and evening.

As my uncle, Mahmood Ali was passing by for a drink, he surprisingly came face-to-face with the Gladiators. Meeting them was as if I was someone famous on the red carpet. I was so excited. Having photos taken with them and leaving me with their autographs.

My room was quite large, leading to the outside garden. The outdoor Wendy House where Mum and Uncle, Imdad Ali, would let me play in the house at a certain position. Constantly holding onto me as I was not yet able to walk. That room soon got flooded and literally washing away everything. Dad, Mum and Tamour, saved my posters just in time.

I was given my own room eventually and it had its own homely feel to it. It had a big heavy brown door and was at the very end of ward nine. Mum added her touches, rearranging furniture and the cards were all neatly hung on the wall. Cards from school teachers, cards from friends, and homemade cards from my cousin, Layla Ahmed, with decorated angels with their unique halos, which I thought was really sweet!

Every morning, a big nurse would force-feed my medicine through a syringe. She did it in such a way that I was gasping for breath. I mean what was all the rush about? I was in tears. Mum would tell her to slow down. But no, she was reluctant and wouldn't stop till I choked myself. I was so angry with her. If only I could move. If only I could talk.

My speech and language therapist really helped me. The sessions were long, but it was worth it. I made gradual progress and eventually was mumbling and sounding words. Pronunciation was never there. On Dad's many visits, he would buy me skittles and Tesco's plastic bowls of trifle. Apparently, this seemed to be my favourite foods.

"Kittllle, kittlllle" I would wail. Telling Mum to scoot.

So confused. She'd rock me so I would eventually get distracted and nod off.

"Kittllle, kittllle," I repeated.

"Oh, skittles?" She finally realised. I would nod. She would then take me to the Tesco's across the road. Letting the nurses know that we were going to be a while.

First Word

There was a test where I had to be brave enough to let a doctor scratch a needle into my spinal cord, this was to help me sit straight and upright. I appeared fine at the development, but soon, the nerves started kicking in. Sitting in Daddy's lap, while mum lifted my top up. Observing the doctor's interactions, examining the way he slid his five fingered stubby paw into the many polymer medical glove, I was fidgeting and was unable to keep still.

The doctor wheeled himself across and thrusting the sharp, shiny needle right through my backbone. I screamed, *"BASTARD!"* and jumped in pain. The room fell silent, amazed at what I said. My first word was a swear word. Mum and Dad were so shocked and so embarrassed at what I had said, nevertheless, they just laughed at the fact that I was finally able to talk!

As my speech was gradually improving and generally making little progress from time to time, I occupied myself by singing.

"Oh dear what is the matter with me?" Rigid and frozen in bed. Eyes wide open, staring up at the ceiling. Or curled up in to a ball, rocking myself.

Once I was fit enough to go to school, I took classes at the James Bindley Hospital School, which was situated not too far from my ward. Mum would get me up and ready in the mornings and a nurse called, Margaret, would wheel me there in my wheelchair. On one occasion, coming back from school, my brother, Tamour had come to visit me. He taught me how to ride my own wheelchair, "Go *forward," h*e instructed. I used both arms to keep my wheels straight. Then he said, *"Reverse for me then steer left and right."* Again, I used both arms to make the wheels go back and then to steer right. I managed to keep the wheel completely still while making a half U-turn to the right and used opposite arms and opposite wheels to make a left turn

Wheeling myself into my room, my sisters, Zara and Sanam, had decorated my room from top to bottom. Zara showed me what she had brought. A yellow toy shaped as a boat, with buttons to press, which made the animal cards pop up. But soon, visiting hours were over, and my sisters and brother gave me a goodbye kiss before leaving. *"Sit, sit,"* I would say. Telling Zara to never leave my side as she was sitting on the edge of the bed. Struggling to get to her feet. *"Sit, sit,"* I repeated, raising my voice. She would then kiss me goodbye. *"You are so clever."* I would call after her and honestly, probably I was right. Seeing how well she has done in life!

I received many presents that I cherished dearly. Uncle Imdad Ali had bought me a Cindy house where Barbie was Cindy's teacher. I loved Cindy's house; it had a teacher blackboard with many coloured chalks, tables and chairs, a literacy and numeracy play area. The children could sit on laid-out rugs ready for story time and nursery rhymes, whereas the numeracy area had coloured, laminated cards with a number on it in bold print. There was messy play too, involving sandpits, allowing the children to make sandcastles and free paint. There was also a little, lime green ball belonging to Cindy's dog. Another gift, which I absolutely loved was a pair of Barbie roller-skates, which were given by another cousin of mine, Nayyar Zaid. Yeah, I know right! You must be thinking why on earth would she get roller-skates for a person who can't even walk? But, it meant the world to me to own a pair of roller-skates.

Tears rolled down my eyes as I lay there. I couldn't believe it. I had always wished for roller-skates and finally, I got them. They were white, with stars decorated all over the shoe in shocking pink, lime green, and lilac.

One warm, humid, and sticky day after school, Mum was wheeling me into my room and my brother was in the far end corner of the room, doodling with one leg raised above the other. I wheeled myself towards him and leaned in to see what he was doing.

"It's a surprise," he said, telling me to go away.

Mum was feeding me a tub of trifle. By the time we were finished and mum had cleaned me down, my brother was done with the sketching. He walked over to me and showed me what he had done. It was a deep, red, beautiful coloured piece of cardboard, with a portrait of my Barbie roller-skates.

I smiled, a wide grin across my face showing my teeth. He then added the last little touch, his signature. He hung the fine piece of art in my bedroom, alone from the rest of the cards. His signature was neatly done in a black, curvy, gel pen with his neat bubble writing!

My Weaknesses

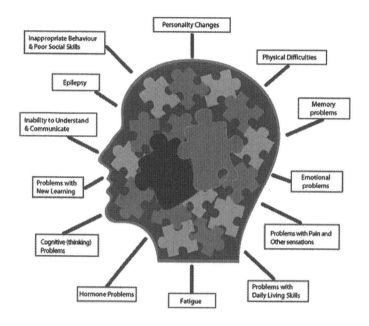

Occasionally, people would have a tendency to make me react. Pushing me to the limits. Despite, being aware of the fact that I do have anger issues, but apparently that's a part of a side effect I have to live with. A side effect to the inflammation. Something I hate.

However, certain people use that to their advantage. I feel the worst people are the ones who cover up their doings, making it look as if it's all my fault. So yes, they use that as a target.

The Tooth Fairy

My front Dracula tooth eventually dropped out. Maria, my favourite nurse, told me to wrap it up in a piece of tissue and to place it under my pillow.

"Don't forget to see what's under your pillow tomorrow morning," bellowed Maria.

I went to sleep really early that night and couldn't wait for morning to come. The next day, I quickly lifted up my pillow to find my tooth in the tissue was gone and replaced with a golden, sparkling necklace. Gold petals, pearls, leaves and roses dangling on either side of the necklace. *"Mum, Mum, Mum, look,"* I shouted, holding the necklace up high so she could see it. *"Put it on me,"* I said, excitement rising in me. Maria had come into my room with a trolley for breakfast round.

"Look, look, Maria. Look what the tooth fairy left for me," I pointed.

"Wow! It makes you look like a princess," she replied.

One night, Mum phoned dad and asked him to collect her from the hospital, so she could go home, freshen up, have a bath and get some fresh clothes for both of us. This meant I would have to stay on my own for a while. She promised me she would only be a little while.

I started panicking. *Where had she gone? Had she forgotten about me?* I thought. It was time for lights out and all the children to go to sleep. *"Sleep time,"* the nurse whispered.

"No," I cried. *"Mummy's not back."*

The nurse continued, *"Mummy's taking a while. Why don't you wait in your room?"*

Nodding like a Churchill dog, my head drooped with tears flowing through my big round owl-like glasses. I wheeled myself back towards my room. It was dark, everyone was asleep. I stopped right outside my door. I turned to my best friends, Joshua and Russell. They too were asleep. I cried and cried trying my best not to make a sound. I felt so alone. A girl in a wheelchair in a big, dark hospital ward. Then I heard the front door being banged shut. I leaped up as I saw two, black figures in the distance, but couldn't make out who it was.

It was my parents sprinting towards me! My face was covered in tears. Mum clutched bags of clothes and loads of packets of crisps. Dad stayed a short while and had to leave, kissing me goodbye. A while later of, watching the small screen television that was in my bedroom.

One of my greatest pleasures was meeting the Princess of Wales, Diana, and Prince Charles shortly before I was discharged from hospital. Their entrance had been so royal with the red carpet being laid out all over the ward. After all, the hospital was named after her. We all gathered around to meet the fine couple and had dinner with them.

They were really nice to talk to and had questions for all of us, like what were our names, likes, dislikes, hobbies and our best bits about life in hospital.

Princess Diana wore a beautiful, peach, floor-length dress that had patterns around her waist. She also had a matching, elegant scarf, whereas, Prince Charles was all suited and booted, dressed in a suit and tie with the black, shiny shoes he still wears after so many years! Fireworks were set off as the royal couple waved goodbye and made their exit!

Chapter 2,

home sweet home!

The night before returning home, the hospital organised a party for me, with banners strewn all over the ward, 'WE WILL MISS YOU' it said, in colourful bubble writing. Balloons were literally everywhere, plastered all over the entire ward and scattered on my bedroom floor.

Mum was standing at my bedroom door, smiling as she opened the door for my nurse to wheel me in. There was a loud, SURPRISE! It made me jump in my chair, forcing my hands to cover my ears from the loud sound of the party poppers. The nurse, who had wheeled me into my room, gave me a hug throwing her arms around me from behind. I glanced around the room, looking at the banners, which were stuck onto the wall. There were masses of balloons, floating all over the floor, which were all a different colour. That night, I was so excited; I was hardly able to sleep.

The next day, at 8.30a.m., I heard the door knock, but I remained in bed. It was dad, he had come to collect us! Coming inside and seeing me awake, he sat on the edge of my bed. Mum was at the far end of the room, still fast asleep. But, she woke up to our murmuring whispers.

The big escape

I packed everything into my bag ready to go home, and I mean everything—my favourite teddies, the blanket, which Maria, my nurse, had sewn for me. The presents I received while I was in hospital, my cyber-pet given by my neighbour, Joshua and the cards I received from everyone. Everything was pulled off the walls. When we got home, the whole street was out ready to greet me. Dad had buggered them off to give me some space. Telling them I was in no fit state to be bombarded with questions. Mum took me inside, carrying me on her shoulders while dad had taken my wheelchair out of the boot.

The big fat Oompa Loompa

Once Inside, Mum put the kettle on for her and dad while, I was wrapped up in a blanket, lying down on the settee. Zara would love my fat chubby cheeks, squeezing them with her weird baby talk. I was as big as a balloon from all the steroids I was put on as a result of not eating. When relatives did come to see me, Mum carried me upstairs with supervision of Zara watching me, talking to me so I wouldn't role off the bed.

My favourite teacher, Ms Morgan from my previous school, ST Francis, Catholic, Primary School. Would visit often, bringing either a milk tray or some nice packets of biscuits. We would love her company and talked for hours. Ms Morgan had an elegant, slim figurer, which emphasised her shape with a pencil skirt and if she wasn't wearing that, she would wear a floor-length dress, which would also show off her figure. Her lovely scented perfume would permeate the room. She had raven hair, in a bob style, which was either, greased back in a bun or let down loose.

She wore black-rimmed spectacles, which made her look smart and intelligent. She was a complete look alike of Whitney Houston!

For the short while I was home, I was sent an invitation by my primary school. I was excited, yet so nervous, seeing my year-4 class teacher, Mr. Jenkins, and my class mates. I remember sitting amongst my old friends was so nerve-racking. Everyone stared at me, asking me all sorts of questions about my wheelchair. *What's this? What does it do? How does it work? Who gave it to you?* I started to cry. Mum, who had just bought me in, called my sister, Sanam down with permission from the teacher. She was three years above me. I now felt a bit more settled, but I still had tunnel vision as though everyone was staring at the broken girl in the wheelchair. I hated it.

The first thing I did once home from hospital, was to have a warm, hot, steaming, cosy bath with my Tamagotchi. Soaking, drowning, and holding it under water. A tight grasp till it died. The water penetrated the insides and killed the poor living dinosaur. Screen going fuzzy.

I cried. Not knowing, bye, bye toy!

I was now fit enough to go to school. Dad had been doing all his homework, searching for the most suitable school for me. My music teacher, Mrs Bain, had suggested that we should consider, Wilson Stuart

Special Need School in Erdington. Dad then arranged meetings with the school head, Mr Collin McClellan. Discussing my needs and my needs regarding my learning. My special needs statement, which was done by the Birmingham Children's Hospital regarding my diagnosis, my fine and gross motor skills, my abilities and weaknesses and many more. And, as a result, I was thrown one or two years back. My illness left me with many issues and one of them was the ability to learn.

Mr. McClellan, explained the schools policy and procedure and their regulations including, the pickup and drop off facility, which was in place to make it easier for families to send their kids to school with peace of mind that they were safe.

"This service has a strict duty to pick up and drop our kids off at the end of each school day, with the dedication and care of both of our drivers and bus guides."

School runs would be expected to be on duty from early mornings. Picking up kids from different areas. School journey's, at the start of the year. I started off in a wheelchair. With the help of the metal ramp, leading me on to the bus where the driver would clamp my chair in so that I don't move. I was then walking aided by a Zimmer frame for a certain amount of time and by the time I was in years eight, nine, ten and eleven, I was walking unaided, where occasionally, the driver would throw racist comments at me. Luckily this seemed to occur only twice, where the bus-guide heard it just on time, told the person in charge of transport and got him fired! Good Riddance…

I remember the racist comment to this day, he said, *"Have you got a bomb stuck under that dress?"* The entire bus fell silent, where only the elder kids and the guide would adopt glances amongst one another. And yet again, I was too dumb to clock on at the time.

I had a wonderful teacher in class 3 named, Silvi Minnie. She was a short lady with grey hair and had a personality like gold!

On my first day at school, we were given a tour around the building, Mr McClellan, my dad and I. After break time, dad left me. The whole class was literally all boys, with just two girls, Sophia and me. Sophia was a really slim girl and was always in a wheelchair just like me. Not using her muscles would mean they may deteriorate over time, so she was made to stand in a standing frame for the rest of the day by the physio. The frame wasn't there to make her walk, but just to stretch her legs, strapping them in. This frame had wheels on each end and brakes to stop her from rolling. However, Sofia had no interaction with me from the day we met. But despite having no conversation with the only other girl, I fitted right into my new school.

Shortly after dad was gone, I was given a class buddy just until I got used to my new school. Silvi announced, *"Nadia is new to this school, would anyone like to show her around?"* A long, awkward silence ensued. But then among the children, a little boy raised his hand.

Brad Adkins had volunteered to show me around. We became best friends. Wheeling my chair around literally everywhere. Break times consisted of small snacks, involving either water or blackcurrant squash with a biscuit or two.

Our playground was not at all very big. It was literally one end to the other end of the garden. Whereas, the big kid playground at the bottom of the field was massive compared to ours.

I would love being outside, in my chair, watching the little kids on their scooters, their bicycles or sometimes when it was a nice and warm day, the children would be allowed to bring their building blocks outdoors.

Eyes would wander down at the big-kid playground. Not just mine but the rest of the children too. I hated being in a wheelchair; it was so boring, not being able to occupy myself except lesson times.

I spent the whole of break times sitting in that chair, watching others enjoying themselves.

Springfield

My years-5 and 6 teacher, Mrs. Cabbage, Nichols was a stern woman, with owl-sized glasses. A short lady with short, grey, shoulder-length, curly hair. She wore dresses with grandma cardigans accessorised with, skinny jeans and plastic, beige scandals. Mrs. Nichols was always in sandals even on a rainy day. She spoke very softly and was quiet intimidating when she was seen telling a child off.

Our classroom assistant, Angie, was always a helping and cheerful character. She had a cute husky voice, which could be loud at times. She always wore either knee-length boots or flat shoes, often with jeans and a top or tights and a dress.

I was still in a wheelchair, but I was now able to stand with a little support, taking little steps. During class, I would sit on an ordinary chair. However, when making my way around, I was put back into my wheelchair.

I continuously had physiotherapy sessions on a regular basis. This helped me tremendously, having a positive impact on my walking. Generally, my strength was improved. Progressing day by day.

Rock and Roll with, Jack Spencer was hysterically crazy. Firstly, we couldn't even dance, let alone perform in the spotlight, dancing and twirling. And secondly the costumes we were told to wear were just appalling. A polka-dotted, royal blue skirt, with a frilly, white top whereas, Jo's outfit was not too bad. A suit, a matching bow tie and a pair of shiny black shoes. Like the outfit you see men wear in, Strictly Come Dancing.

When I made it to year-7, I was walking with the support of a walking frame. A new pupil started our class, Russell Plotneck, A lively and cheerful character. The first day he arrived, he observed me from afar. He took big leaps towards me, his bulky shoes thumping against the smooth laminated floor.

He muttered, *"I know you. You're Nadia. We were in hospital together."*

Neighbours, exchanging Conversation. He was a good friend of mine.

My class tutor, Mrs. Anne Cradock was a lovely lady with a great sense of humour. Not only was she our class teacher, she was also a PE instructor. She was very enthusiastic and dedicated in what she did. Organising many activities and events such as, the Queen's jubilee, where each pupil had a choice to wear either, red, navy blue, or white. Mrs. Cradock often dressed rather casually—tracksuit bottoms, navy fleece, with the school logo printed on the top, right breast pocket with bulky, white trainers.

Russell Plotnek, Brad Adkins, Chris Vowls, Kyle Hall, Jack Spencer, and me would all look forward to our mobility sessions, which took place two days a week. Physical activities would be arranged by, Anne with the help of physio's to improve our balance and stability.

Activities would involve, walking along the straight, narrow bar of the back side of the bench. Both feet touching. Maintaining balance. Exercise mats, exercise balls, gymnastics, paddling boards were also used, where we would lie on our tummies to improve stamina and strength around the waist and pelvic area. There were wheels on either side. We pushed ourselves in this position, which made our hands rather filthy. This worked our stomach muscles. Supposedly tightening them.

I was now walking unaided from the help of both physiotherapy and mobility sessions.

Taking full advantage of swimming helped me a great deal. Teachers would love my laugh. They would say it's like a loud, booming, ear-piecing chuckle, coming from deep within the throat yet so cute. I don't understand how that can be cute, but oh well!

Mr. Collin McClellan was due to retire that summer. We prepared him a book, full of memories and achievements from year-7. Collin's assembly was very emotional. Both the specially prepared book and the assembly, itself was stocked with achievements from all years, primary and secondary. He then spoke a little about what he was planning on doing next once he had retired. His previous role as head was handed over to, Mrs. Audrey Trunchball. Audrey was a tall, slim woman with short, grey hair. She spoke very politely, however, she could change within seconds. Harsh, abrupt and quiet stern, requiring close observance of her students. She was blunt and intimidating. Nothing like Mr. McClellan.

My year-8 teacher was called, Mrs. Kitty O' Brian. Kitty was a lively character with a great sense of humour, until she became deputy head in 2006, despite being the most loved form tutor. She was always livening the place up. We had enjoyed the company of Kitty very much. Being in her presence, she was more of a friend than a tutor. Her nickname for me was, Glad Nad's…

Kyle came up with a slogan, *Nad is my dad and she drives me mad!* And he repeated it throughout school and the first two years of college! Frigging annoying!

I met a girl called Nadia Hoda; she was two years older than me but yet so immature. She always smelt like chocolate. Not the good kind, but chocolate which melted in the sticky heat. I hardly knew the girl, but according to her, I was her new best friend, just because we had the same names!

"Oh I was born before you, so you copied my name," she would say.

"Ugh, who are you?" I retorted.

She would literally beg me to be her friend, scaring the hell out of me. A regular stalker. She would follow me around, wanting me to hang around with her. She would wait outside my classroom door each day, walking me down to my bus. Apparently, we're cousins. Well, that's what she would say to everyone.

What the hell, why would she say that? It put me on edge. She would see me in the corridor from afar. I would run away from her before she had a chance to see me. Despite everything, I did feel for her. She had no friends. But I felt as though she would bully me if I stood up for myself. I felt she was forcing me to socialise with her. She had a bad reputation, stealing from her fellow class mates—mobile phones, school equipment, a computer mouse and so on. The police would speak to her in the head's office.

Steven Hudson, the new head teacher and Ratatouille Turvey, Year 10 Form Tutor was also present. Mr. Hudson, had blackish/ grey hair. He was always dressed in a suit and a tie with Clark's Smart and sophisticated office shiny black shoes, which dad always had regular discussions about.

2006- School was now a sports college.
Wilson Stuart School and Sports Colleges.

Russell's biggest fan was Shakira.
He always carried it everywhere he went.
Laundry Service
Her Cover Album
In his big black backpack, which was thrown around so many times that the colour eventually came off.

It was no longer black, but a dusty grey colour.

Plugging himself in. His tatty earplugs
Listening to the CD literally everywhere.
In Registration, on the boom system, on the bus going home.
And Pauls Radio. A DJ. On at every break times.

In the (SRC,) sports hall
Organised by Tyler Turall with the help from Leah Gibson.
Part of Priestley Smith. Deaf and Blind School.

I would ask Russell many times if I could borrow the Shakira CD and he'd be like
"No, but you can listen to it during class."
Russell passed away. Year 2003. Aged 13-years-old.

Unaware... he left the CD for me in his will. A Memory of him! The entire class broke down in tears. I remember. I remember it as if it was just yesterday. We were all sat down. Registration had just begun Kitty came in. Not being her usual jolly self. *Hang on... What's up?* I was sat opposite Brad. Instead of going straight to her desk, Kitty propped her elbows on the table where I was sitting, leaning, forcing all her weight on it. *"I'm sorry class b... but I have some terrible news."*

We all looked at one another, stunned at the tone of voice she was using.

"Last night, Mr McClellan received a phone call. And I'm devastated to say, that Russell has sadly passed away."

The room fell silent, taking a moment to digest the sad news that was just imparted. Tears sprung to my eyes and began streaming down my cheeks. The entire class was in bits and cries of the children echoed around the room. We had been so, so close. Hospital buddies and now class mates, but he was gone now – gone forever.

Brad, who was sat opposite me, his face wet, drowning in tears. He looked at me, giving me a smile... a little supportive nod. *"It's going to be ok,"* his voice trembled. Taking me a while to return the smile.

We were supposed to be performing a play. The Berewolf Play, that very same day. In front of our families. We did not have time to grieve, it was too late to cancel the play. Kitty thought it would be best if I was given Russell's script. I did know him the longest. I refused. Reading out Russell's bit in the dazzling spotlight. Mr. Plotnek looked up at me. Chin shot up from his lap. Through the mic, my voice became wobbly. I couldn't do it. My lip started to tremble.

The next day, in registration, Russell's CD was on the teacher's desk.

"Huh, that's odd. What would it be doing here? I thought.

"Nadia, can you come here please. I have something to talk to you about," asked Kitty. Tucking my chair in, I very slowly made my way to the front of the desk.

"Russell left this for you," she informed me. Her voice was about to break, clutching the CD in her hand, her eyes watery. She continued, *"Russell's dad came in this morning. He wanted to give it to you in person. He was too upset. So, he left it with me"*

I didn't know what to say. Instead, tears ran down my cheek.

"Don't cry bumble bee," she said, wrapping her arms around me.

"Thank you," I muttered quietly.

Back Home, at my cousin's house, Kabeesha was there. She made me feel awkward as usual, with her sick and twisted comments.

"If you ain't got nothing nice to say, don't say it, simples!"

She was constantly looking down to the CD in my hands, eyes wide and curiously looking steadily with a fixed gaze. She was seemingly admiring and fascinated by the rigid square shaped object.

"I hope you weren't looking forward for him to die, so you could have that CD."

I was gob smacked. How could anyone think like that? My eyes began to water. *Oh God...please no.* I was angry and humiliated, my voice breaking up.

*"I can't believe you just said that." I said. W*alking off. I stomped into the living room and demanded her daughter, Yoyo to take me home.

"Stay for lunch," she insisted.

"No, take me now. Otherwise, I'm leaving," I shouted.

"B-but what happened?" she asked.

"Ask your mum that," I replied.

I would imagine she wouldn't have had the courage to ask. On the stairs, doing up my laces, Kabeesha popped her head around the door—cackling.

"You're silly, you are."

Later on back home in my bedroom, my cousin, Layla, who is a year younger than me, texted me, *"I heard what happened. Are you okay?" she asked, concerned.*

I replied, *"Just because I'm disabled, doesn't mean I don't understand."*

She muttered, "Hmmm?"

She then came over, to read the letter I wrote to Russell's dad:

Dear Mr. Plotnek,

Sorry for your loss!
We are all so, so devastated.
Furthermore,
Thank you for the Shakira CD, it was much appreciated.
Listening to it makes me think of all the memories we shared.......being in hospital as well as our time at school.
I cannot imagine the pain and grief you and Mrs. Plotneck are going through, but today we heard the entire class broke down.

We lost someone close to us
I now hope that you and your family have all the courage to move on.
It's all a matter of time.

Kind Regards

Nadia Khan.
Xx

We never did know what happened to Sophie. The girl who never spoke to me since the day I started school. The only other girl in class, I felt as though my confidence had gone through the window. Time flew by and still no sign of the missing girl.

Year 4... No Sophie.

Year 5... She still didn't turn up.

Year 6... Still no Sophie.

Year 7... Where the hell is she?

Year 8... Still didn't show herself.

Where could she have possibly gone? Some people say she passed away. Some say she stopped attending and others just didn't have a clue.

If she had passed away... would teachers tell us? I doubted it very much...

We were so young and naive.

Summer 2003

Kirsty Gillian, sweet and friendly. Loud, funny, enthusiastic and lively with a great sense of humour... just like me!

Real. The total opposite to Nadia Hoda, that's for sure. Kirsty was friendly whereas, Nadia Hoda, was Jealous and a vicious creature. Only mingled with me. Purely for time pass. She was rude, arrogant, and self-centred and if she didn't get her own way, she would swear at you. She always tried her hardest to split Kirsty and me up.

Mission impossible, "There is no way I can come between you two."

She would say, *"You are in the same class - always seeing each other."*

But no, Nadia Hoda, was eventually able to keep Kirsty and me apart. Stopping us from seeing one another on our breaks. So, we created our own little hide-out. The back exit of Mr Turvey's classroom!

I would always sit, thinking things over and over again. Going mad over the same thing. Questions floating around in my mind. Lost. Unsettled. An emotional wreck. There was always an urge to burst into tears. Forcing back the sting, burning at the back of my eyes. Unresolved questions constantly spinning abruptly around in circles, but yet, there was never a single answer.

Why me?

What have I done so wrong to suffer this?

Why was I disabled and no one else?

Why am I so slow at processing information?

Why am I here? A place where literally everyone was in wheelchairs and yet my condition was not as bad.

Why is it that the people who get it bad, constantly struggle the most?

I was frequently at Kabeesha's house quite a lot. Not because we had become close. Never... but I wanted to spend time with her kids. I could never predict the atmosphere or the nature of their moods, but despite, the constant bullying, we did have a good time, however, I guess that was an excuse. Becoming close to me so they could manipulate me. Getting me on their sides. To brain wash me. Prompting me. Forcing information out of me. I was used as an easy target. So stupid. Being a dumbass to fall for their game. *Man...I do regret it!*

Singing became a daily routine on lunch breaks. Our Singing practice was run and taught by a professional musician and vocalist from the Symphony Hall Orchestra named, Sally. We started off with warm-up techniques and exercises specifically designed to train our voices, so that we don't strain the trachea or damage our voice boxes. We sang In acapella, without instrumental accompaniment. And at other times we used our voices to emulate instruments, harmonising the pitches of various keys of the piano. *La, la la la la la la la la...a sequence starting from high to low.* What a wonderful world by, Louis Armstrong. Performed at the Christmas concert. Adeding our own beats, rhythm, and pitches. Maarya Jabeen and me collaborating and sharing the various solo's amongst one another. Either Duets or a Solo.

I have taken part in singing publicly in many venues, including: the NIA, (National Indoor Arena.) The Symphony Hall, the Vodafone Presentation and Celebration Evening. Where the BRMB presenters hosted the show, awarding me with HMV £50 vouchers and the head of Connexions, Martin Flynn introduced the show. The school Christmas and summer concerts. Where, originally, I started performing from year-eight onwards. Either a solo or a duet. And finally, year-11 karaoke night, at Butlins. (A leaver's trip.) Catherine Dass, Faisal's career. Would doll me up for these concerts. Dressed accordingly. She would apply the suitable makeup and style my hair for these occasions. On lunch break. I would change into my dazzling concert outfit in one of the cubicles.

I would run to my classroom where Cathy would have her curling tongs plugged in. Her makeup bag and everything spread out in front of me.

My year-9 tutor, Sandy Kinvig-Madame Kinvig to us. Yes… she's from France. She was also our French teacher and actually thought I was good enough to go and practice my French in France. She recommended it in my school reports.

Nadia should have the opportunity to practice her French in France as she is a pleasant and fluent French speaker! Well, back then, I was anyway.

Now.... I still know the vocabulary and pronunciation, however, I have since lost the French annotation and affection.

During my years, ten and eleven, the class was divided into groups. 10.1, apparently, being the most intelligent. Me, Kirsty, Kieran, Matthew, Lee, Faisal, Scott and Ben Macqueen, were all in one group. Our classroom assistant was, Margo O Regan and Ratatouille Turvey, class tutor. Whereas, 10.2's group tutor, Anne Millie with two classroom assistants. George and Julie. Another student was added to the group. Aatish Mumtaz. Annoying and so Immature!

Couldn't stand the guy! Food and Tech classes with Pam Mackenzie were awfully messy and yet so fun. We were split into groups. Me with Kirsty and the boys... well they would always cause a scene on who was with who. Throughout our times cooking, we would make all sorts of appetising foods. While we prepared all the ingredients and utensils. Pam always had a thing about licking the spoon. I don't know why, but, anyway as we were all cooking away, I just couldn't resist the smell. Holding the spoon over the sink, I would take a quick lick, especially, of the cocoa. Making sure

Mrs. Mackenzie had her back turned. Everyone but Aatish would always *grass on me.*

"Ah, I'm telling," he would say.

"No Aatish," the boys would nudge him a little too late.

Eid - our religious festival. It's tradition is to wear dazzling clothes, exchange money and to go around visiting people's houses, filling our tummies with delicious and appetizing food. It could be a bit boring to be honest. Well, I remember that Eid as if it was just yesterday. On the morning of this eventful occasion, the routine was, for the men to start off the day with their rounds, with the Eid Morning prayer at the local mosque, and then they would pop down to our house for a little get together, eating, talking, and laughing!

Once they had all gone, we were upstairs getting all ready to shine. I was sitting on the edge of the bed sorting out what jewellery I was going to wear that day. Kabeesha swung open the door, ranting and raving and accusing me of all sorts! Apparently, I'm doing something that is not easy in our religion. I wouldn't like to say what the accusations were because it's not even true! So pathetic, so immature – giving me a bad name! My patience was tested to the limit. What does she really want with me? She shouldn't be accusing us of this shit. The truth is,

Kabeesha should be looking around elsewhere. *What goes around comes back around.* I've seen it with my own eyes. But who would believe me... a silly little girl who doesn't even know anything. That's what she thinks of me, no values, no standards, just a broken abnormal girl. Eid was cancelled because of her screaming at the top of her lungs and upsetting my family as well as me.

My Art teacher, Mrs Chrystal Rowland's. You know those softy people you get when they're always in cuckoo land. Well, she is one of them. A bit like my aunt DP. One of my art modules was 3D designs. We were told to fabricate a 3D animation design of a ghost. Once we completed the process of creating the ghost, we then added our own features and functions. I used Microsoft Publisher to generate the illusion of a Casper-like ghost. I made use of a programming technique made available to me, which allowed voice and movement. My ghost was a contrast of our art teacher. It was a clumsy ghost. Dopey and stupid.

It had a husky, cute voice. I implanted movement so it could wave and introduce its name, filling the screen with its see through skin and bang its head against the screen glare.

"Siik, did you make that?" asked Brad.

"Yeh, it's the C.R ghost," I replied.

"What does that stand for?" he queried.

"The Chrystal Rowland's ghost," I said.

All of a sudden, between laughs, I heard a shriek. I turned around only to find Mrs Rowland's in tears.

"But…but," letting out an ever so high pitched bawl, which no human ears can tolerate. She ran into the corridor where she could have some alone time which, completely, threw me off guard. So unpredictable, unexpected and unanticipated as, I thought she would have went with the joke, but apparently not.

Meeting Prince Edward and Sophie, his wife and the Lords Mayor and his wife too, was absolutely phenomenal! It was so exciting to meet our royal guests. They were accompanied by the police, and their presence initially frightened the primary children. We had the union jack as our theme. Both dinning bays were smothered with union jack flags. The primary kids waving them about all over the place. We were dressed accordingly to match the flag, red, blue or white. Prince Edward was afforded a grand entrance. He was accidently hit on the nose with one of the flags while he was bending down to a primary child in a wheelchair, named Olivia. The princes visit graced the front-page of the, *Daily Mail* newspaper - an epic article dominated the whole page.

I liked the fact that they were so normal just like you and I. They didn't once boast about how high-class they are compared to us. Prince Edward told me how he and Charles would argue at times. Just like any other sister or brother who argue like cats and dogs. The entire car park was crammed and overcrowded with police cars and police motorbikes. The gold necklace in which, the mayor wore, must have been worth tons as I could hardly keep upright wearing that heavy thing!

People would constantly ask questions about my pain, about the fight I constantly live with and, the day-to-day struggle of pain and, whether I like it or not. They would come across as, sounding, rude, abusive, bad-mannered, vile, obnoxious and, so ungracious. But, there are ways and means of asking a question. Not bluntly and candidly spitting it out, sounding rude, ungrateful, and aggressive. Assumptions and judgments really piss me off.

My youngest sister, Zara, was admitted at the children's hospital with a diagnosis of Meningitis a few years after my illness. But unlike me, they caught her bug instantly, so she was able to get better, making a full recovery. She's normal, with no disabilities and no deformities whatsoever! Seeing her in hospital scared the shit out of me. Having a blanket over her legs and stripped naked with her finger being lit up by a blue LED light, looking like ET... thin as bones.

Time flew! Final year. Year 11. A class project based at the Vodafone. The teacher involved in all of this was, Mr Andrew Buxton-our science teacher. And what a lovely bunch to work with! The project lasted two weeks and the ones who actively participated were awarded with a certificate and a ceremony at the Town Hall. The achievements were awarded and announced. I was to perform on stage, singing, '*Where is the love,* 'by the, Black Eyed Peas. Monique, a Vodafone member, joined in with the chorus. The room fell silent. A man from the BRMB station came on stage and said, *"And now to introduce a special member of the show, Miss Nadia Khan. Everyone was c*lapping and cheering me on. A moment of panic took over me backstage with Mr Buxton.

"I can't go out there, you've seen the crowd, there's millions," I winced.

An encore greeted me,

"You can do it! I believe in you… we all do. You inspire people."

I got up, attempting to hold back my tears, which were trailing down my face. The curtains swung open and the audience were clapping and cheering me on. The stage was so bright. Monique appeared from the audience at the beginning of the chorus and I broke out with a huge grin. Exposing my white teeth. I could just about make out the BRMB presenters sitting at the front with, an outline of Mr Turvey, standing right at the back of the audience, watching—leaning against the door .

Dove dale National Peak District Park in Derby. A geography fieldtrip with Mr Damien Jackson. To cross the river, we had to walk on the stepping stones. Kirsty, me and Cathy thought of going first. The water was freezing cold, so cold - enough to kill. I felt a little nudge on the shoulder. I lost my balance and as I was slipping, I felt my foot losing balance, sinking under water.

We were all asked to do a, Practice Mock Interview... applying for a Classroom Assistant Position. Interviewed by, Linda Grattidge. She was pleased with my performance and gave me positive feedback: Nadia *was smart and appropriately dressed for the interview. Her body language was tense to begin with, but became relaxed during the interview.*

Non-Verbal Communication: Nadia was very good with maintaining eye contact. She did occasionally use some arm/hand movements, but not excessively, just to emphasise points.

All in all, Nadia spoke very clearly and her tone of voice was just right. Not too loud or too quiet. Answering questions clearly and kept to the point.

This candidate's interviewed is good enough to be considered for a post. Nadia didn't overuse her catch phrase (ain't it.) Very Well Done, Nadia.

I was appropriately and sophistically dressed to kill in a suit and a jacket. A white collared shirt with titch buttons with buttons running down the centre length of the entire clothing accessorised with a greyish two-piece, a blazer and boot-cut trousers. Very office-like.

School dinners were the best! A van would deliver the healthy meals while the cooks would prepare it. Toilet breaks were in between and at the end of lessons. Twenty minutes before lunch time, going back to lesson, we had to walk past the dinning bay. *Oh the smell was just scrumptious! I was eager to know* what was on offer for dinner. I would sneak a quick glance behind the cook's hub where all the food was being prepared. It was so busy that I couldn't even see past the cook, who was frying, draining the oil, baking, mixing, heating and, so on. As the second bell rang, we knew it was dinner time. Second-helpings were always on offer. But I would take it before finishing the first! Ensuring I got extra before it was all gone. But obviously, once the dinner ladies had seen what I was doing, they'd tell me I can only have seconds if I finished my first serving. But, by then it had obviously all gone. My appetite had increased. My taste buds had gone wild. I was eating a lot more, but I was slim, very slim – like, a size zero.

Our end of year residential trip: Butlins, Bognor Regis. A year-11 farewell residential do, before we moved onto our own bigger and brighter future plans. This was my first real holiday away from home. Full of memories. Summer 2006. Butterflies robbing the insides of me. So...so... excited! So much so, I thought I was going to be sick.

First day, on arrival, we unloaded our luggage. By mistake, I set off the fire alarm thinking it was a light switch! Everyone ran outside. A man in a uniform, in charge of the holiday resort, came running out.

"It was a mistake," I apologised. A grin forming across my face.

He said it was fine and not to do it again.

"Trouble Maker"... teased Paul

"On our first day we arrive and still, you're up to no good!" he joked. Sarcastically I walked off.

Early Morning. At 6am, I woke up to a roar-like sound. I thought there was a lion outside my bedroom door. Jumping out of my bed, I tiptoed, just to find that it was the sound of Mrs Minnie and Melanie snoring.

At twelve midnight, Mrs. Minnie, Melanie, and George all took me to the seaside while the boys were fast asleep. It was a warm night with a cool breeze, so dark, I couldn't tell the difference between the sky and the sea. The border amongst the horizon was all one colour, dark blue. Its surface reflecting the colour of the sky, making it look like one big galaxy. It was an incredible sight and one I will never forget.

Parent's evenings at school were always in the late evening, where all my tutors would be gathered in the sports hall. They would be sitting at their tables and discussing my progress.

The more good feedback I received from the teachers, the more eager my dad was.

Mr. Buxton and dad spent literally the whole time talking about the cricket matches that were on the night before. It's fair to say my parent's evening went well! I passed my GCSE's. Woo, woo! Regardless of the preparations and the long-ass revision nights, I didn't expect to pass even one of my GCSE'S let alone six! I did really well in all of my favourite subjects: Science, Geography, English, Art, French and Food Tech. I failed maths, something I would attempt to pass in the future...

But, later on during higher education, re-sitting maths wasn't as easy as people thought it would have been. They constantly nagged me to get it quickly done and out of my life. Others would tease me, saying I'm dumb and slow and that's why I can't pass it!

That wasn't the case at all– number one...

My coordination had gone and dictating everything to the scribe had made it 10 times harder. Though I had extra time it was never enough. Slow and Irritating. And number two: I was told that I am most likely suffering with Dyscalculia in Mathematics. A severe learning difficulty that causes problems in learning maths. Trouble making arithmetical calculations as a result of brain disorder, which makes it harder to make sense of numbers and maths concepts. So to people who thought they knew my ability and weaknesses. I think not! People should concentrate on their own lives instead of controlling and focusing on mine!

Mr. Collin McClellan has been head teacher of our school for nearly twelve years and still talks about the happy memories of the achievements of both students and staff. Since leaving, he still works part time as a special education consultant and finished with this in 2008 when his wife retired. He has kept himself very busy with two allotments where he grows his own fruit and vegetables. Also, he helps organise a folk festival every year.

Anne and Tim Cradock retired in 2002, though they continue to work for the disabled, taking part in fundraising charities and volunteering for many disabled sports. They arrange outdoor events worldwide and still continue to hold various disabled sport all over the world including, being boccia officials at the Paralympics in London, 2014, being a wonderful experience.

Andrew Buxton had left in 2006 and moved to Wales with his family and, Ratatouille Turvey retired in 2014, but still continues to teach maths at the school, two days a week.

Chapter 3,

Wings to fly!

Last goodbyes and final farewell. Independency. Responsibility. Decisions on future ambitions. Either continuing with education or lazing around at home. My initial plan was to go away to Hereward College in London. A residential Institution. Catering for people with disabilities. Hereward provides a lively, stimulating, intellectually and demanding education in a friendly and well-disciplined environment. While offering on site student accommodation blocks. Also maintains its independency and assures minds are motivated.

Dad and I paid a visit to the college. We took a tour around the main campus and housing arrangements. Masses of people with all sorts of disabilities and specific needs.

Its environment was very similar to school. In that learning was broken down into small groups. Making it easier for students to learn. Grasping, absorbing, following and, understanding.

Decisions. Decisions. Decisions…

I now stuck to JMC, in Erdington. (Josiah Mason College). Choosing to stay local. A mainstream Institution, and Wilson Stuart Sixth Form for the first three years of my time being there. Duncan Lynes, Wasiq Hussain, Melissa Williams, Hayley, Zaair Rehman, Brad Adkins, Jerome Smith, John Collins and myself. Our TAs: Pitbal Millhouse Eileen Cookbook and Beverley Hills. Josiah Mason. A huge building.

Extensive and widely spread. Thin and narrow as a thread. Long narrow, small in width corridors. Limited and inadequate.

My first chosen area of study was the Cache in Childcare. Modules involved consisting of various assignments and tasks, which would be required to be ticked off in order to commence the next step: Personal Development, Human Growth Development from birth to old age, Food and Nutrition. Health and Safety Practices in the Home and Group Setting,

Care of Children, Play and Practical Activities and The Orientation to Work Test Paper.

Second half modules included of: An Introduction to working with Children, The Developing Child, Safe, healthy and nurturing environments for children, Children and Play. Communication and Professional skills within childcare and education, The Childcare Practitioner in the workplace and finally, An Introduction to Children's learning.

My Friends... Zubi Pour and Nazneen Noora were studying the level 3 in IT. Their classes were a flight of stairs above ours. We became really close and were literally together all the time.

At home, sitting at my workstation with my assignment loaded on the computer screen. My phone started to ring, showing no caller ID displayed. I rarely accept unknown calls, but the thing is, this time the caller wouldn't stop... constantly ringing straight after each call, barely leaving a single break in-between! Basically, scaring the shit into me. I answered on the third ring. I was nervous - my voice shaking.

*"Hello" there was s*ilence, no reply...

But then, a deep and croaky voice revealed itself. *"I know who you are and I know where you live."*

My heart started racing. My eyes scanned every corner of the dorm. The room was spinning, a hot flush sprinted up my spine. *Who could it be?*

But then, as I was going to end the call, the person started to laugh. Panic struck me. I recognise that cackle, this ain't no stranger, it's Kabeesha. I was annoyed and vexed. Feeling resentful, I swiftly ended the call. The next day, Kabeesha was unable to keep a straight face, mocking me, "*You sounded soooo scared!*" she said.

I guess you can call me a trouble maker when all I wanted was to be treated like everyone else. A Rebel! I would long for the freedom of my peers. To be allowed to wander off campus, but the remaining time I was still a Wilson Stuart pupil. It was agreed to keep a close eye on me for safety issues. Having my best interest at heart. This was quiet hard for me to understand as I was still only in my teens. Being so naive. I would perceive it as, they're doing everything possible. Stopping me from socialising with my friends rather than seeing it as my benefit. It is a cruel word out there! Nevertheless, despite being told many times, I would still tagalong with a friend. Going to the local shops on lunch breaks with them. Finally, three years flew by and I was no longer a Wilson Stuart pupil, free from their overprotective grasp over me, once and for all.

I would love interacting with the children. Developing a close bond.

Literally every morning, the children I was working with, (Pre-school) would run up to me shouting, *Miss Khan, Miss Khan,* throwing their arms around me as I would struggle to get through the door!

Ruksar Baig. A fellow class mate, also working in the same setting, but with the babies. We would meet up on lunch breaks. Going outside to catch up on work or just to chill out together. One day, we were going to the staff room. We both sat down, putting on our coats... ready to go to the chip shop.

"Careful Guys," a member of staff interrupted.

"A vicious dog is let loose in the area. Just stay clear," she advised us.

"What?! I exclaimed. My voice trembling. A shiver running up my spine...a tremor, making me feel cold despite the warmth. Ruksar was reassuring me although she was agitated herself.

"Don't worry, we'll take a short cut," she suggested, nervously taking deep breaths to calm herself down.

"What the hell, Ruksar... we hardly know the area and you're expecting us to take a short cut?"

We slipped out of the nursery gates. There was a steep path leading up to the main road, almost like a hill. Nervous and scared, our legs literally lost, shattering, giving way beneath us. Finally, we got to the top. Slow in deadly suspicion and scanning the road. The dog, just two doors away from the footpath of the nursery. My voice barely a whisper. Quiet enough for mice to hear. *"Don't make a sound, even if the dog looks at you, do not show that you're scared....trust me, dogs can smell fear from a mile away."*

A thought then struck me. *I'm the one who walks clumsy, not her. He will hear my footsteps and come charging towards me.* And that's exactly what happened. I took a first step. The dog was lying on its front saw me and galloped and charged towards me.

"Run!" screamed Ruksar.

*The dog was l*eaping and jumping. Barking uncontrollably. Finally we got to the end of the road. We were so relieved that he was no longer there.

"Phew," I said. While we tried to catch our breaths.

I let out a victorious sigh. We ordered a doner burger and chips. I was not so keen on making our way back.

"He's gone," squealed Ruksar.

"Don't keep your hopes up," I muttered, expecting the worst to happen. The dog was out of sight, out of mind till, the bottom of Alexandra Road

"There he is," I whispered... The dog was laying on its front.

"Let's find another way," said Ruksar, shielding herself. She took small steps hiding behind me.

"This is the only way! We're nearly there now. If we were to take that shortcut, it'll have to be the opposite end of Ali's chip shop and there's no way I'm walking down there again."

We continued with our baby steps. Drained out, one, the heat and two, avoiding that bloody dog. Running for our lives and rushing our way back towards the nursery gates. He started barking aggressively, using his mouth to get a grab of our clothing. Ruksar had no problem. She reached the gates in no time at all. It was me, as usual. Breathless and wheezing. Full of sweat. Fighting off the dog with my clumsy and retarded walk. Panic. Red in the face.

And then... I threw my burger at the dog. It went flying. Making a run down the hill. Hoping that my ankle-length boots don't give in... gliding flat on my back. The dog had a little nibble on the burger, but then continued to chase me. I was sticky and hot. Tears and sweat rolling down my face. *Any minute now I'm going to slip.* I didn't. The next day, a member of staff told us that the dog had been captured the night before by the police, they were running wild. Apparently, chewing a little girls face off. You monster!

That day, Ruksar and I were eating in the staff room, we were on our lunch break. There was a comb and a one pound coin on the table. An Afro-Caribbean girl from the baby room was brushing her kinky hair, textured and frizzy. She was combing her hair away from the scalp allowing it to extend out from her head in a large rounded shape, much like a cloud. She then realised the coin was no longer on the table and began to throw a fit. We all stopped eating and looked on in amazement. She pinned the blame on us. Ruksar and I continued to rant and rave, screaming her head off. My mouth dropped. We were so speechless. She was ruining our reputation and giving us a bad name.

I shouted, *"Listen yeah, why would we want a pound if we have our own money? You do see us going to the shops every day and if you're dying over a 'pound, I can give you one."*

She then reported both of us to the nursery manager. Those two weeks were literally like hell. Dragged on for ages as if time had come to a stop. News had travelled ever so fast and everyone saw us as thieves. No one would talk to us and, if they did, it was only because they had to. We would sign in, do our business and leave without saying a word. Until, two weeks later, at Alexander House Nursery, during the children's playtime, she found her coin under the table in the staff room. Camouflaged with the colour of the carpet.

"I found it, I found it," she screamed excitedly.

"You shouldn't accuse people of doing such things then should you? But only with proof, you

can think about blaming people." Said Ruksar. She was then told to clear our names. The nursery staff sincerely apologised for the irrelevant accusations.

I then went on to a placement setting at, Marsh Hill Primary School, In Erdington, Birmingham. My Supervisor, Ms. Gaynor Milliver. Our class teacher, N. Roberts, managed the classroom, with a wide variety of skills and techniques used to keep her students and pupils organised. She was orderly, focused attentively on each task and academically productive during a class to minimize the behaviours that impede learning while, maximising the behaviours that facilitate and enhance learning. I worked with a class aged, 5-6 years and had to keep a regular, Reflective Practitioners Diary, which included my experiences and the observations/activities I had to carry out.

I was now to choose an appetizer, one year course, BTEC First Diploma in Computing and IT. Charles Adams, my personal tutor, kindly sorted out my enrolment forms, giving me an interview. I presented him with my recent certificates proving that I am capable of working at that level and the intensity of work load would be manageable for me.

The mandatory units that were required were: Using ICT to present information. To understand the purpose of different documents and the basis for selecting appropriate software. Presenting and communicating information. Commonly available tools and techniques in application packages. Reviewing and adjusting finished documents. Introduction to computer systems and the different uses of computers at home and businesses. Being able to explain and discuss the use of common types of hardware in a computer system. Selecting software for a specified user and safely connecting hardware devices. Configuring the specified software. Website development. To understanding websites, the law and guidelines, which may concern their development and the principles relating to a multi-page website design. Being able to create a multi-page website. ICT Supporting Organisations and database software. Involving the structure and principle of databases, being able to create a database to meet user need. Creating database queries and to document it. My spreadsheet makes use of a range of formulae, functions and features, presenting analyse and interpret data involves checking and documenting a spreadsheet solution. Doing Business Online. How businesses use IT. And the end of the year, believe it or not, I was the only person in the entire class to pass, gaining enough grades to progress further as the rest of the class were literally too laid back, interested in making chit chat and, relying on my help.

They are as follows: A Levels in Computing,

(IT and Business Practitioners) 18 units in total. Nine in the first year and, nine in the second.

Communication and Employability skills: To understand the various job-related attributes. Technical skills, and knowledge needed for that specific job. Working procedures and systems as well as planning and organisational skills. This is to assess Time Management and specific skills within each individual.

Computer Systems: The Essential Hardware supporting software intending to use. Breaking a computer apart and putting it back together.

Information Systems: The source of information and its characteristics, identifying the internal and external sources. How organisations use business information and operational Issues.

IT Systems analysis and design: The Development Life Cycles, Development Mythologies and the investigation and analysis process.

Communication technologies: Discussing the various Communication Devices etc.

Organisational System Security: The Potential Risks to ICT systems and Organisations.

Access causing damage to resources and Website Defacement.

Principles of Software and Design: This includes Legislation and its Professional Bodies. **IT Technical Support** and **IT Systems Troubleshooting and Repair:** Discusses the importance of help desk, desktop support and remote support where the user connects to the client machine, attempting to resolve the problem.

IT Systems troubleshooting and Repair: The suitable remedies to repair IT Systems, applying false remedies to Hardware and Software Systems. Explaining how organisational policies impact on diagnosis and repair, applying good working practices when working on IT Systems.

E-Commerce: The effects on society. Implementing the technologies involved in E-Commerce, explaining its security issues in E-Commerce and the law and legislation guidelines that regulate it.

Impact of the use of IT on Business Systems: This unit explores how Hardware, Software and Systems are forever being developed.

The class was a majority of all boys. Hussain Mesnani, Madyan Rahman, Saad, Patrick Mensa, Jabaar Hussain, Ahmed Abbas, Fat Lard, Yasir Abdoo, Yusuf, and robot. With three girls including, myself. This is probably because, more boys are likely to go for this subject and tend to choose the technical issues of IT whereas, if girls were to pick this subject, they would most likely prefer the social and creative uses of ICT instead, of the other.

Our Form Tutor, Faye Dixon, was loved within our group. A popular member of staff with a great sense of humour. But yet to any new person, she would seem harsh and uncompromising. While we were new to the course, I remember being shit scared of Faye, but then again, I think we were being overdramatic. I would imagine she would have come across as hard to push her new students.

"Faye expects a lot of work," I said. *"We might as well not hand in our coursework, she will only fail us without looking at it twice. She will fail us just because we used a full stop when we weren't supposed to."*

""I'm leaving," cried Hussain. *"She's such a strict teacher. Her pass criterion involves* so *much. It's like a bloody distinction."* Faye was the best teacher we ever had! We just seemed to misread her. She was an amazing person. Considerate, caring, and always willing to go that extra mile to help her students achieve the best grade possible. More of a friend than someone to just mark our work!

I stopped visiting Kabeesha's house for good since the day she successfully and slyly got my friend's number and prank called her. A practical joke... she assumed. Expecting me to pick up the pieces the very next day. For some odd reason, she didn't like that we were so close. *As if she had a say.* Lisa Bennet was a member of staff, Faisal's career and Kabeesha did everything in her power to stop us from being friends.

CD, manager of IT. Would send me to Zubi's every mornings. To wake her up for her 9:00 clock start. Not being quiet fully aware of my walking. Well, obviously, I wouldn't have told him. Hiding my disability. I was more than happy to go just as any normal person would. Plus my walking was much steady and better in those days. Once at college, both Zubi and Nazneen would run to Zubi's for cups of tea during our lunch breaks. Golden Fish bar was the hype back then. A chippie near the college. They were the best chips ever! Not like any other chip shops where they would use sweet chilly for the dressing. The chips were so fresh too. We would run to the chip shops, rushing back, Zubi would peel the chips off the paper for me using her fingers so eagerly.

I find it difficult to doze off. I never switch off. Feeling groggy almost all the time. There's never a time where I've had a good night's sleep. Just Like a baby does. I would rise to any little sound, so light like the feature hitting the ground. The dragging of feet against the downstairs carpet, the shaking of a carrier bag or the sound of a page being turned. My mind constantly on record and over thinking things through.

No wonder people say I'm losing it. A neurological problem. Rejecting any sleeping pills the doctors would offer me, guaranteed to make me feel drowsy in the long run. Shutting off anywhere and at any time. My mind always plays tricks on me. The times I actually want to dose off - it always wins, never giving in. From each class there was two people picked at random, nominated as class reps. They would have to attend meetings, voicing our opinions and speaking on behalf of the class.

Coincidently, Hussain and I had been volunteered. Names were picked out anonymously. The first meeting involved the reps, managers and senior managers. One of the main concerns from Faye was that there was not enough hard drive space. Downstairs, in the lounge, the room was packed.

My Nerves were starting to kick in. It was my turn to speak... Uh oh,

I could hardly make any sense of what I was trying to say. *Tap... tap, "Faye, hard drive, no space."* Tapping on Hussain's shoulder, telling him to ask for more hard drive space.

Speedily, striking his shoulder, *"Faye hard drive, no space, Fred hard drive, no space.*

Faye hard drive, no space." Snapping back, he would say, "Bloody hell. *"No... you've got a mouth, just say it."*

Saad would always make fun of my walking. Constantly chanting *fall, fall, fall."*

Either he knew he was making fun of my disability, or he was too blind to see. Once, I was so wound up, I said, *"Say it one more time and then watch."*

He repeated, *"Fall Fall Fall."*

I lost it. I flipped reaching out for his hair. I pulled his bushy afro hair and in my hand I found a hairball. I had ripped a chunk out.

The way I wish to be accepted in society is for nobody to notice the way I walk and if they do, they should be gracious enough not to say anything about it. Instantly, accepting it with no questions asked.

Eventually, Faye had no choice but to tell the class about my *disability*. I hesitated of course, but she was so adamant that she should inform the class, seeing as my reaction earlier had been so appalling and, atrocious.

I did eventually say, *"Okay, you can say I have a walking issue but, don't use the word, disability,"* She agreed, but did anyway. Making the word, 'disability' sound so obvious. I was so embarrassed that day. Wanting to disappear.

Certain family members would talk to me as if I was a baby and somehow think to themselves that it's

OK. Apparently, getting away with it. Assuming that I hadn't noticed.

How can you not notice? Talking down to me in the way that is not acceptable to me.

It is humiliating and patronising. The awkwardness of it all, makes me feel uneasy, fidgety and, so nerve-racking.

I loved my English classes. They were so funny, yet so lively. We had two teachers,

Kyle Morris and Hope Chapman. One for literature and the other for language. It was a mixed group; we had students from all sorts of classes. There was a PowerPoint presentation. This was to present a slide show on our dream job. Being the first one up to deliver. My nerves got the best of me, yet again. I could feel my nerves tingling, like being tickled with a small feather. The anxiety curled into my stomach. My hands became sweaty and the thought that I've tried so hard to forget, wriggles into my mind.

Anxiety crashes over me and my every waking thought is consumed with this worry. Soon, what was once a seedling of a problem, blossoms into a sturdy oak tree. My jaw clenches. My hands make fists. Palms moistened. Blood rushes to my ears and I feel hot.

My pulse skyrocketing and I feel my face becoming hot. My eyes slowly sliding away from the zombie like faces in front of me. With my staggered, robot-like movements and Limbering stiff neck, I literally broke the computer, which was used to project the slides onto the interactive white board. Smashing it to the floor. A crowd of laughter echoed around the room. I felt so small and so embarrassed.

Chapter 4

broken

Final year. We moved to Birmingham Metropolitan College - Matthew Boulton Campus. This was an all-round, glass building, nine stories high with a wide range of courses available.

We had no choice but to move colleges, since the school opposite our college, Stockland Green wanted back ownership of their land. The college was In the City Centre. Zubi and I, would make regular trips into town.

We would go into the Bullring Shopping Centre, linking arms along our way, with intertwined, enfolded hands. If ever we weren't connecting arms, I would most likely fall to the ground! The sudden rush of adrenaline as I let myself go, my knees giving way beneath me. Hitting the ground, my limbs twisting over one another bruising my legs. Gradually, my walking was slowly deteriorating. The difference in my ability from then and now was massive.

Second year A Level modules... **IT Project:** (A double unit) a lot of work to pass! Recognising the Project Specification, Project Lifecycle, Test, Document and review the IT Project, examples explaining why projects fail and discussing the different tools and methodologies that are available to the project manager. Various phases of a project life cycle identifying the project and collecting the required information to producing a project specification.

Advanced Database Skills: Describing the purpose and features of a relational database, design and implement a working relational database, with five tables and to set up relationships according to the user need. Design and implement data entry forms to ensure its validity and integrity of data.

Advanced Spreadsheet Skills: This is where we had to create a complex spreadsheet that is fit for purpose and to check its accuracy. To use formulas and functions and, to solve complex problems. We also had to summarise techniques to interpret a complex spreadsheet using chart and graphs to present data graphically and to meet a define user need.

Client-Side Customisation of Web Pages: This was where we had to describe the implementation styles of CSS, showing how it's present in HTML, to discuss the main features of the chosen scripting language and to design, create and test web pages using scripts to implement its interactivity.

Human Computer Interaction: Describing the impacts of HCI in recent years on each of society, economy and culture, the fundamental principles of design.

Event Driven Programming: Discussing the key features of event-driven programmes and improving the user interface and functionality of event driven programme based on its review.

Website Production and Management: We had to produce a website that is W3C compliant. To design a multi-page with two-way interactivity and to consider the factors, which impact the website and to discuss the security issues ad legal constraints involved in websites.

Digital Graphics and Computers: Evaluating the impact of evolving output media on the designing aspect, file format and, compression techniques.

Computer Animation: Where we had to discuss how persistence of vision is used in animation, and, creating our own animation using programming techniques. Networking and so on.

One of our lessons with Faye, was a two-hour lesson. This was our last period of the day. At break time, I was overcome by a condition… reflux as well as a swallowing condition. Multiple conditions known as Dysphagia and Dysarthria. Effected by Ataxia. The muscles needed for chewing and swallowing in the same way that, other muscles may be effected. Caused with either a brain injury or brain stroke. Easily prone to choking. The muscles around my throat are weaker than most peoples. Needing full attention. I would go to the speech and language therapist for this. Sitting near the window, I threw a sweet as thin as a love-heart into the hatch. A circular, lime-green sweet, which had chalked on powder smudged all over the sweet to give it a hint of flavour. Distracted from the outside world, the sweet slipped down my tongue and into my wind pipe. I started to violently gag, which made nasty noises as though, I was going to throw up. People around me started to look. *Shit, what do I do? There's no member of staff around.* I was hardly able to catch my breath, catching my passage of the gorge. I start to wail, leaving its sour flavouring as it grazed against my oesophagus. I thought I wouldn't survive! Panic struck me, I was all choked up with its powder, gasping for breath. Thinking any minute now, I'll pass out. I must have looked like a right dumbass running past the double doors, stopping for the open window with my unsteady balance and gait. Feeling hot. I stripped down to my sleeveless dress. I was gagging violently. The contraction of the back of the throat triggered by the object being pushed on my trachea. The Laryngeal Spasm. Tears flowing dramatically down my cheeks, while I was choking up in powder. I gave up. *There's no way I can fight this,* I thought! The noises of people were now drowned within me. *Don't give up.* Taking all of my strength to find myself. My throat was numb and stinging from the sour taste. *You can't give in.* Making my swallowing muscles work. Closing my eyes full of tears, I got myself to swallow hard and with the last, concentrated, solid gulp, the sweet was able to slide down my trachea, leaving an active trail of its substantial smoke. Choking as my throat had a stiff grip of its powdering taste. Instantly, I poured down my orange oasis to sooth the strong and heavy aroma. It didn't work…

The days Zubi would come out and link arms with me, a day in the bullring, we would go shopping and then stop off for a bite to eat. People would make nasty remarks. Looking me up and down and giving me dirty looks. Once, there was a tall, slim, black guy, in the City Centre, eying me up and down. *"You?"* Commanding me to come forward. I was planted frozen amongst the crowds, glued to the spot. Watching him, mimicking the way I walk. As he mocks me, legs planted apart as they bend at the knee and my knees flexed. Taking large leaps as I sway from side to side with my head constantly at a fixed position. He let out his hideous and awful cackle. Stopping my bottom lip from breaking out into a cry, pushing back the already fallen tears. I was determined not to let him see that he got to me. I was looking at him full of rage, eyes watery, I said, "W*hat goes around, comes back around." My v*oice was breaking as I walked off. He threw me a confused look. Turning on my heel, I Joked, *"look it up in a dictionary."* Narrow-minded and so Immature.

My family has changed quite a lot. Previously, we would all be together, making decisions and discussing stuff and literally being together all the time. And now..... It's as if no one cares. But, generally the way people's perception is nowadays it would be... *I'm better than you are and I'm better than you.* Who cares? They'd boast about how bright their sons and daughters were, but when it's us, no one gives a damn. Honestly, I did think to myself that probably it's since the Pakistan people migrated and mingled with our lot, but no that's not the case at all. Society and humanity changed. People only think about themselves. A dark, brutal community!

I'd get picked on from certain members of the family, for no particular reason, no names mentioned. And to top it all off, they're so egocentric, arrogant, selfish and unmindful to think about the fight in which I battle every single day. The daily struggle of pain. But no, apparently, it's them and them only. Heartless, wicked, and beastly! Attempting and succeeding to make me feel uncomfortable with their signs and motions. The awkwardness of it all... and the worst thing about it is, I take everything to heart. Thinking, *why did they say this? Why did they say that?* Thinking things over and over. If only I could brush it all off. Their negativity. With the shocking and appalling comments. But no, instead it sticks and clings onto me like a strong and powerful glue.

In the event of a fire, there was procedures put in place for the disabled. However, not for me. As we were told to evacuate from the 7th floor to the ground. The adrenaline of crowds of students rushing to the stairs, causing my vision to go all blurry. Despite trying all my best to remain close to the grab rail, exposing my white knuckles. Gripping to the bar as tight as I could. My palms all sweaty and moistened. And the thought of tolerating this claustrophobia and clusterness soon ends. I attempted to keep my feet as close together as possible. Taking small steps at a time. People were knocking me and this would usually send me flying. On the 6th flight of stairs. I lost it. My vision going blurry. Everything going round in circles. A foggy mist clouding up my entire line of sight. I was tumbling down the staircase. Laughter ringing in my ears. The humiliation of it all hitting me *smack* in the face! A hot flush trailed down the length of my back. Tears cascading like a waterfall down my face. One of my lectures barged past everyone to help me get up. I felt a pain radiating through the back of my head. Pounding and Banging. It must have been from hitting my head against the sharp corners of the steps. That's one thing I hate about MBC - their staircase has no carpet!

During lesson, Hussain and I would have a weird urgency to check the price of Britney tickets online on her official website. We'd be hyping like crazy until, *"Look Hussain,"* I pointed, tucking my chair in closer. *"Look at the price." I said. "Flipping hell!"* Annoyance in his voice. Presuming it would be £40 for her tickets! Zubi and Nazneen had now gone off to Birmingham City University to complete their final honours year in Computing and IT. However, Zubi, for personal reasons, soon dropped out. However, regularly we would meet up for a catch-up, have a meal or take a trip to the cinema.

Below is my personal statement, written and amended a few times, when applying for a computing course at university. After meeting the requirements, having more than enough UCAS points to get onto a business information systems course. I was then accepted, but unfortunately, I had to turn them down as my coordination started to rapidly and increasingly, deteriorate. Of course, I was disappointed! Disappointed at myself. I had my whole future ahead of me, but then what can you do when the thing stopping me from progressing is out of my hands? I guess there is nothing left but to accept. It did take me a long time to move on, but occasionally, it does upset me. I did get there but within a flash, it was all gone. I no longer had it.

Personal statement

There is a tremendous impact in the IT industry as newer technology is constantly being introduced and as a result in this, I am very interested to learn about these changes. It was my IT teacher, back at school who had inspired and encouraged me in IT at a very young age. Subsequently after, I had always been intensely involved in operating and functioning with computers, which are the most dominant and influential tool in my life. I would like to continue with my studies as Iwould like to develop, further in my knowledge and understanding and to also, improve and elaborate on my skills. The reason why I have chosen to apply, further in computing for IT and business is seeing as, I have always been a determined and studious individual. Hence why, I knew that a degree in which, I had a lot of background knowledge in, university would be the next step for me as I have a broad interest in computing in IT. In particular, the reason behind my choice is the complexity, challenging and intriguing nature of the subject. Furthermore, I particularly enjoy the way in which, business and IT blend in with every day issues. I have a fair amount of knowledge and understanding of how computers operate and make a major impact in the music and entertainment industry. I am currently on an A-Level programme, in IT and business. (IT and Business practitioners) And this consists of the required modules and unit which are: Communication and Employability Skills, which are valuable skills needed within a working environment to be an acceptable employee within society, Computer Systems which included me learning about the required hardware and software and various compatibility devices relevant to a specific operating systems. Organisational Activity consisting of how organisations use the Management Information System, etc., organisational system security, e-commerce, impact of the use of IT on business systems, IT System analysis and design, communications technology, principles of software design and development, event-driven programming and Computer Animation. The optional modules, which are considered are, IT project, advanced database skills, advance spreadsheet skills, client side customisation of web pages, human- computer interaction, web server scripting, website production and management, installing and upgrading software, digital graphics and computers and object-orientated programming. The skills in which I have gained learning and understanding throughout my current BTEC course is, that I can actively perform an installation and a backup, I have learnt the importance of backups and the legal threats that may damage and corrupt data, how to create an interactive dynamic website with the implementation of a scripting language such as JavaScript. I have also learnt about different operating systems and their requirements, the effective skills and attributes needed within an employee, hardware and software utilities and various devices and physical change within an organisation, relating to the use of IT. The modules, which I believe show my potential ability and progress is e-commerce and website production and management. I have also been nominated within the class for being a class rep. This involves me having many responsibilities such as, valuing all members of the group's views, comments or concerns and sharing them with professionals. Issues raised may vary and there are no certain aspects of college life to be discussed such as the health and safety of others, whether the college is clean enough, the introductory of new facilities and many more. I have been a student/class rep in the previous year, 2010 and am looking forward to continue with this responsibility in the next academic year, commencing, year 2011 I also completed my A-Levels in Computing. (IT and Business practitioners)

Kabeesha, always bombarding and putting me down yet again. Always resenting the fact that I wanted to continue with my education. *"When are you planning on leaving college? Are you going to study for the rest of your life? You've done every course possible. Some people are just not meant to learn."* Sarcastically, she would say, *"What's it to her?"* My bottom lip started to tremble. Stomping to my bedroom, my voice breaking, *"Why do you always put me down?"* Cackling in Response. A shrill, broken manner.

People have been known to react. Now they've seen what I went through, they take every little thing as something big. When a member of the family is not well for instance they would comment,

"Oh no, she's going to become like Nadia."

"Oh no, she's going to become like Nadia." My adrenaline crashes. The fright and terror. *"What the hell man?"* My voice raising and a serious expression forming across my face.

"Your daughter is just fine." I said. *"Just because she's ill, doesn't mean its bloody Encephalitis. Don't go comparing every illness to me!"*

Year 2011, our final year. Hussain and I had been selected to represent the college. However, it did not occur to us until after the six-week holidays that our pictures would be used globally for all Metropolitan Campuses. Plastered all over the college…

The Image above is taken from,
The Matthew Boulton Website.
(With Hussain Mesnani left.)

My worst paranoia starts when people would stop and stare at me. Having nothing better to do than to look and mock at the way I walk. But it was actually one day when a member of staff said to me,

"Don't you ever think to yourself that they might be looking because they recognise you from the website, brochures or the college prospectus? It hit me then, when I was at the subway.

Opposite the college. A group of college students who I have never met in my life, approached me and said, *"Are you on the MBC Website?"*

"Yeah," I nodded. A smile gradually forming on my lips. Only then did I realise as I made my way over

to my table at the opposite end of the room near to the window.

On our end of year trip to Alton Towers, I had to pay for both Saad and myself because I accidently broke his cap, which apparently cost thousands. *"Fall, fall, fall."* Infuriating. So immature and unsophisticated. I couldn't help it. *He must be aware of my walking issues, it doesn't take a genius not to know!* But regardless, he still decides to torment me. Persisting with it. *"Fall, fall, fall."* Testing my patience. Letting out a sigh of frustration as my eyes burn into the computer screen. Hearing his irritating sarcasm. Lips tightening into a fine, grim line. *"Fall, fall, fall."* I lost it. Blood whistling in my ears. Sweat trickling, oozing, pounding my bones. A faint hiss of disappointment. The sudden urge creeps up hitting me violently. Instantly I seize the cap. Placing it back in its original place. It was a shitty New York Yankees cap. Worth a couple of quid. But the way he bellowed after it was as if he had lost a grand.

As my gawky walking increasingly continued to get worse, I no longer had a say in having my independence, but I was given supervision whether I liked it or not. I had a support buddy with me literally, everywhere I went. Dad accompanied me from the college car park to the reception area where a member of staff would meet me. The staff member would then take me from one classroom to the other. A burden on everyone and so embarrassing for me.

To any stranger, I acted as if I had a wonderful, perfect life. Covering up the truth - the messed up life in which I have. A prisoner in my own home.

"Oh, she's got problems with walking so let's wrap her up in cotton wool. Hiding her from the outside world. OK, so I do have a walking issue. (A hazard to myself if I'm honest.) Doesn't mean my freedom should be taken away from me. It just means I have to be that extra careful when I do go outside. *Well durr… wasn't that the reason why I got a wheelchair? To socialise, to get to know people, to join activity clubs, to occasionally do my own shopping.* But no, I'm stuck in the house, living with dad and gran. As I deteriorate, rot away, fading, easing off and diminish till I vanish. The Little Prisoner. Going mad with the same old shit. Thinking things over and over. No wonder people say I'm losing it. I can't work, I can't go out to meet friends. Nothing. Well technically, I can, but only under supervision.

OK, let's be honest, my independence has still been taken away from me in my early 20's than when I was a kid. Probably, all down to my parents looking out for me. Sometimes coming across as being too harsh and protective, but that's down to the fact that they generally care, although, it may also be due to trust issues. The fear and doubt of letting me roam the streets alone where presumably they may think that anyone and everyone could use my walking as a sign of vulnerability. An easy target.

One of the conditions I am left with is, Cerebral Atrophy, which is obviously the disease of the brain and involves the decrement of the size of cells and loss of neurons in the cerebellum, the area of the brain that controls coordination and balance. Deteriorate and die. Cerebellar Ataxia, (ACA.) is when the cerebellum controls gait, muscle movement and, coordination, becomes inflamed or damaged - A stiff neck. A Cerebellum Disorder. (Cerebellum Shrinkage) A rare disease: Medically, they would say. Brain Disorder.

I've always known I wasn't certain people's favourite, but what really pisses me off is when, they actually started to show me their true colours since the day my parents split. Probably it's because I choose to stay at dads. Who knows? But I can see it in people. They resent the fact that I'm only a visitor at mums and choose to stay at dads. And the days I do stay at mums, I dread telling certain people. The fear of them thinking, *"Wow, she's staying at mums today."* As if I've done something good; *"Chill your beans.* There's nothing shocking about that!"

My depression had gradually got worse and worse. The more stuff I would bottle up and hide from my family, the more stressful it got for me to hack. If I did do something about it back in college days, it would've gone by now. But taking up counselling would have meant going through shit to resolve my problems. Saving the hassle of explaining myself to others, had become a problem. The fear of people lacking in patience to listen to what I have to say. But instead, rush, and, hurry me. Leaving me, being, nervous, speechless for words and, angry at how bloody slow I am! My stupid slurred speech. I do understand, but it just takes me that extra bit longer to process my words.

Family genuinely believe that, no one is known to be clever, but only the ones with a university education. The one who's passed a university degree with flying colours and continue to do well in life. The one, who's earned their respect, are the ones who have good stable jobs - that's me out of the picture then! I learnt my lesson the hard way! University was my dream. I admit that. But, regrettably, I couldn't pursue with it, because of medical reasons. My Destiny I guess! And, because of that, the people who have been through it, virtually everyone, don't look at me twice. Apparently, thinking, I have - no values and I am unworthy. I'm unintelligible and unmeaning to them. Purposeless and hollow; well, according to them that is. I have a lot of pressure to live up to, unlike, my friends who don't have to live with this stress, day in and day out. Intellect, isn't all about university, the way people think it is, I know this now. But, it's the person as a whole and, their wellbeing that counts. OK, they may prove to be sharper by talking more sense on particular subjects. They are faster and clearer, but, I say never underestimate everyone else. Just because I don't engage in discussions, doesn't mean I don't have a view. I'm not dumb (as people would say.) Just because I'm slow, doesn't mean I don't know what I'm talking about and just because I haven't been to university, doesn't mean I'm any less sharper and motivated than the people who have made it. I notice everything, good or bad, I just don't speak on it.

I do shy away from walking and walk as limited as possible. The name calling, the stares, mimicking and the nasty facial expressions sometimes become too much to bear. In family gatherings, I stay sat in one place, amongst other bodies, while all the young people have left the room. This does upset me. Until someone looks at me, I then, whisper or mime, *"can you help me please."* And only then, will they take me out, holding on to my arm so I do not to fall - I hate my walking. It's the one thing I feel that is so obvious. I don't like relying on people either.

I was now given a wheelchair from, West Midlands Rehab Centre where I would go for my occasional appointments. The wheelchair was given to me for long distant walks or shopping trips. I was more than happy to use the wheelchair as it was way better than my retarded walking. But as usual, I had to get used to the people always staring as they gaze fixedly and intently with their eyes wide open. I found it hard to accept and ignore as they would look directly through me, until I would blink or turn away. I thought it was very rude, disrespectful, and so brusque. I thought to myself, people would obviously stare more if I was to walk without any sort of aid and lurching from side to side with knees flexed, taking big steps. My weird and stupid balance obvious for all to see. So, for that reason only, I had to de brave enough to go in to a wheelchair. Still, ensuring that I use my legs for most of the times.

Chapter 5

Driving has been a wonderful experience for me. Scott Dent, my instructor and disability advisor at the RDAC. (The Regional Driving Assessment.) I was referred to the RDAC, driving for my disability by the mobility centre for an assessment and within this assessment, I found that my condition will have a tremendous impact on my ability to drive. I was able to read a standard number plate at a distance of 20 metres. My adaptations, which were considered by, Scott himself. Which, stated that I drive in an automatic car where the foot controls were now hand adaptations. Steering was functioned with my right and for my left, a floor mounted accelerator, where, pull is to accelerate and push is to break or to come to a stop. During the assessment, I drove a

Nissan Note, automatic transmission and because of accuracy of foot placement was poor, paddle action was then investigated while the vehicle was stationary and with this, my performance was much improved. I then, trailed hand controls with the right hand and, faired remarkably well when asked to set the engine speed at specific revolutions. Scott and I agreed on a vehicle, which featured a floor mounted Menox E with an accelerator and break. Designed to be operated with the left hand. Tuition was now considered, which was owned by the assessment centre as there were no other instructors in my locality that have, my required adaptations and for that reason, the Driving Advisor, Scott Dent, was prepared to work with me, out of office hours as he is no longer an instructor, but a driving advisor for the disabled.

I was now, accepted on a Psychology course at Birmingham City University. I was very much looking forward to, learning how behaviour impacts a person's wellbeing. A week before my start date, I received a phone call from my cousin in Aboyne. *"I heard you got a place at University,"* she teased. A pause… *Congratulations,"*

"Oh thank you," I retorted. Silence. Poison, caressed like a cool breeze, counting the seconds. The shaking of limbs, waiting for the sound of an explosion of voice, however, there was nothing but

a long awkward pause... *"Nadia, how old are you?"* Her voice was cold... I didn't answer. *"You do know, we are only one month apart. I'm in my final year and funnily enough, you're just about to start."* I was fuming. Anger was rising within me. Why is it always about competition when it comes to me?

Within a flash, my entire life had been changed. I was no longer, the same person I used to be. I had many sacrifices that now formed a part of my life. The many barriers and the things in which I now can't do. Stopping me from being independent. My physique being the first. Of course, my life hasn't gone as planned or the way I wanted it to, but hey, that's life I guess.

I had dreams, but unfortunately, because of my stupid condition, I couldn't fulfil them, often tending to blame myself for it... I still fight for that *dream,* thinking that eventually I may get there - but who knows? Coating myself with negative thoughts each day! Fulfilling my destiny, isn't straight forward, as some. All in all, typing up my autobiography, has been lengthy and yet therapeutic while the emotions, which were bottled up, anguished, began to rise to the surface.

My mind, fractured, and destroyed, becoming my own disease. A side effect. Trapped and lost, in my own, negative thoughts, Brain dead. A fortunate miracle!

Solitary and alone. Abandoned and blanked out. I shy away from people and avoid family gatherings. People disregard me despite the fact that I talk to almost everyone. They would act as if I'm not there. *The unwanted burden.* Ignoring my presence. I'm Invisible to people. Probably, my presence doesn't grab or hold people's attention. I don't know, but... people tend to pay attention to whomever, or whatever, naturally grabs their focus. Like the ones who stand out, projecting themselves full of confidence. Parking me to one corner. Ignoring me conversely. The low self-esteem, letting people treat them like a doormat. Walking all over them without thought or regard. That's me! Perceived as the one who shouldn't be spoken to. The one loser, only hang out with. They think I'm dumb. Brainless, dazed, dense and dopey. Simple minded, and slow.

In one ear and out the other. Tough as nails I am, but... *shhhhhh, no one knows it.* I see myself as being intelligent just as any other person would be. I did ask my relative, JJ once, *"why do you lot, always ignore me?"* His response, *"Who do you think you are? The queen or something?"* I laughed it off, but after that, I kept quiet. Never bringing it up again.

They're quick at jumping the gun, often blaming me for being the moody and arrogant one, when really, all I'm doing is giving them back a taste of their own medicine. *Ignore me, and I'll ignore you back… simple as that!* But apparently, when it's me cutting them off from the group, or constantly blanking them, they don't like it. They assume me of being a snob. The unpredictable, temperamental, emotional and touchy one.

Instantly, people judge me as causing hate to the ones who disregard me. Hates a strong word. The truth is, I don't hate anyone, but instead I distance myself, saving me the hassle of being all uptight in front of people. I feel nervous and quite down when others do ignore me and, act as if I'm not there. The odd one. Making it obvious, when I am at people's houses. They would either, talk amongst one another and leaving me aside, or they would park me alone on one side, while they were chatting, or playing away. Making no effort, whatsoever to include me.

I do think the world's against me. They see me as lacking in a way that they are not. The boring one, who doesn't know anything. I ask them a question and a moment later, they look away and continue to chat with the other person and the excuse I would get is, *"Oh I had something else on my mind."* But that only seems to happen with me and no one else.

It's as though, being *disabled* makes me invisible, giving others an impression that I shouldn't have a say, to be inconspicuous, and only good for just sitting there. My tears began sticking to the insides of my lashes. I think people only know one thing - winding me up. Just another way to get a reaction from me. Having many physical difficulties and inner disabilities means, I am no different to others. I may be a bit slow and require needs for specific things. I may take much longer to do things, but in the end I will always get there. I always feel as though I may have a distinctive disabled look. Inheriting strong features or something, but apparently, I'm wrong. Diagnosed with Encephalitis. A brain stroke. Aged seven-years-old. This forever changed my life. Deceit and Puzzled.

I currently suffer from a number of physical deformities, short-term memory problems, emotional problems, ongoing pain, and other sensations. Fatigue, daily living skills, and difficulties with cognitive thinking and processing of new information, inability to understand and communicate, (slurred speech) and, poor social skills. I choose who I get on with. *Well what do you expect, when literally everyone blanks me out?* Hiding my disability from others. Friends, family, strangers. *It's easy for people to say, I should be like this or I should be like that. Not knowing the inns and outs!* I vow to never let my disability get me down but - who doesn't have bad days?

Why trust anyone with what's going on in your life and fear being judged? I avoid telling people about my disability and the many conditions that I have. The terror, fright, and anxiety of what they may think of me. Friends, teachers, strangers, college, and University Professionals. I see myself as an embarrassment! Useless and pathetic.

There are many things, which I can't do, either life itself or me as an individual. And these things, affect me the most. *Emotionally - I'm done. Mentally - I'm drained. Spiritually - I'm dead. Physically - I smile!*

People have been known, to be so judgmental. Just because in the past, I may have shared a bad experience with them or a time when I was feeling down. Most likely having a bad day, but who doesn't have down days? Even normal people have good and bad days let alone me. Nevertheless, based on the fact that I tell people, assumptions are made that I'm ungrateful, unappreciative, and just so ungracious. But in fact, I am the total opposite. I'm actually proud of my life. Despite having to go through a lot each and every day. Taking life and embracing it because, there's some people out there who have it a lot worse.

I do have good and bad days. Times when my walking is at its worst, and other days when it's not so bad. Then there's my crappiest days, when I feel absolutely shit, not wanting to get dressed at all, my hair remains dishevelled and all over the place, and I just think things over and repeatedly. *When will my struggle ever be over? In a big fat mood.* The constant battle that I have to fight every day. I do occasionally have my rants, but it's never to the point of not appreciating what I have. My depression kicking in - Hysterical, Incoherent, Ludicrous and unperturbed!

Receiving a protection of statement from, Birmingham Local Educational Authority. Statemented with special educational needs means, I am slow, taking that extra longer to grasp information, requiring additional time to complete things. I do have needs, but who doesn't? My needs, are specific to me. I guess, getting through my A levels without additional support and no help whatsoever was an achievement for both me and my college lectures!

Through my life, either the illness itself or, the aftermath of dealing with the many side effects I constantly and successfully hid. The fear of being ignored. Hiding my feelings. Constantly bottling them up as it affects me. And, if I choose to say something about it, I'd be seen as an attention seeker. Keeping in my feelings. My emotions, battling to rise to the surface. Bottling them in as people park me to one corner and because of this, and the way people treat me, I avoid and distance myself from people. It saves me from all the stress and the fuss –not to mention the awkwardness of it all. People would drop their insult and as I take it personally, they'd say, that it was nothing but a joke, hoping that I wouldn't realise. *As if… how can I not know the difference between, being all serious, mocking, all uptight and, a joke?*

I have a strong commitment in whatever I do and never wanting to give up. Ensuring and making others are aware that I'm no different to anyone else. Ignoring the haters who put me down. Kabeesha and cousins. *Keep trying and eventually you will get there!* Stephen Hawking.

Paralysed as he is, never lets his difficulties become a barrier as he eternally and positively pursues in what he does. He is my inspiration. He never lets appearance and impressions stop him from what he does! A role model to people with disabilities! Suicidal thoughts had got to me bad. Assaulted by the sights and sounds of what had been. From the realisation that I may be capable of something so unforgivable. I have difficulties with learning, progress, and development. I would always compare myself to the people around me. I still do. Despite knowing everyone is unique and different.

People would always look at me a moment too long. Aggravating me.

Physically and invisibly, I'm changed and I don't like that. Francis Titchen, (Learning Support Coordinator.) Made me realise, *A disability is much easier to accept and move on for the one who is born with it rather than getting it later on in life like me.* As they don't know anything better.

Writing this book took a number of attempts. Amending, chopping and changing, modifying and altering. Writing this book is my desire to influence and inspire people who have given up hope, either with a condition or not. To make a difference to someone's life. Especially to people who have gone through a similar condition to mine. Keeping in mind that people can never stop you from living your dreams, keeping that motivation going! Doing what you love. Dwelling on education, with commitment and motivation was what I did, but my problem is, finding it hard to accept my *disability,* which would make my life ten times better if I came to terms with things. A barricade!

I was tormented, picked on, and, bullied by Kabeesha literally, all the time and despite the urge to fall for her trap, I never did let her win. She meddled with my school life, my college life and my home life, when really it was none of her business. She would ask me questions. Questions always regarding me and what I was planning on doing. *"How old are you? When are you thinking of giving up college? You've done every course possible."* These questions did piss me off, but what got to me the most was, how she would know everyone's date of birth off by heart. *"You're this age and she's that age."*

Having everyone's age and date of birth programmed and registered in her head. This would just annoy me to next level. After years of terrorising me because, according to her, being disabled meant that, I shouldn't do anything but just to sit at home and, doing what I loved vexed her big time. *What the hell has it got to do with her?"* Despite, getting shouted at from people to back off and leave me to it after all, it was none of her business but still, she was so persistent with it and only stopped picking on me when I did quit with education, the time my condition got worse and only then did she leave me alone – evil and twisted!

I tend to walk knees flexed and posture slumped, unsteady, and liable to fall. Extremely anxious about tumbling outside of my home as people around would usually laugh and jeer. In college, I would remain near to classrooms, avoiding the busy parts. Often sacrificing food or drink for that entire day. The fear of dropping something and drawing unwanted attention to myself. Isolating myself. Reluctant to admit openly to peers about my physical disability. Finding it hard to talk about. An embarrassment! People see me as lacking in ability.

Everyone that is. But my motto is - *eventually, I will get there*. Taking that extra time. Learning, absorbing, following, responding or processing and understanding new information. Another thing I don't get why. A freak with a hidden disability!

Ignorant People. Lacking in knowledge. So cruel, the way they mock and laugh at the things which are obviously out of my control. It's hard to explain to someone who has no clue. An invisible illness. It's a daily struggle, being in pain or feeling sick and broken on the inside. While looking fine on the outside. I had no choice but to become immune and used to the sickening comments people would make. The mimicking and the way people would pull horrible faces at me. Presumably funny. What would tick me off the most is, how strangers would ask my parents about me, and not to me. Ok, probably when I was in a wheelchair. I'd be kind of ok for people to ask my parents but now, I guess there's no excuse. People would still act as if I'm not there. *"Oh, how is your daughter now? Does she still have problems with her walking? What do the doctors say?"* Thank the Almighty

"Uhh hello, I am here, you know!" Linking my parents arm, I would usually look the other way. Act as if I didn't hear. People would tend to ask my mother. Somehow thinking that it's normal to ask. I would imagine it's because mum would answer all the questions being thrown at her. Ignoring my wince, telling her to stop – I would find it so embarrassing!

As if, living with a chronic illness isn't hard enough. The daily struggle of pain, the medications that, either don't work or I can't afford. The side effects. The sleeplessness nights. All these things that I don't have a choice but to just accept. But, there is something else I am living with - GUILT. I'm holding onto the fact that I can't do what I used to do. I depend on others now more than ever. I am unable to do what I should, and because of that I'm afraid loved ones will resent me… The constant hospital appointments get to me more than anything. Waiting rooms, smelling like a synthetic death. The florescent lights glared on tiled floors. Waiting, I witness many sick people. Some upset as they are bored, those waiting are sad, yet impatient and mad. Diverse and crowded. You could practically feel the worry and sadness coming off of the people. I don't mind it as much, it's just getting up for a frigging Neurology check-up. The same old thing, usually telling me to walk up and down across the room, a number of lapse. The finger to nose test or to check my reflexes. Telling me what I already know - I'm getting worse. Rapidly deteriorating and losing touch sensation. My balance going downhill. The constant referrals. Cerebellum Shrinkage. *Blah, Blah, Blah... Blah, Blah... Blah, Blah, "Your CT scan show, you are not improving." Tell me something new, why don't you?!*

Kabeesha has forever, been so negative. Always putting stuff into my head and attempting to brainwash me. To despise certain members of my family. *They did this... they did that.*

Rubbi*sh!* Tormenting me 'Big Bully!'

I do enjoy reading, and I read for pleasure, which increases the obvious, higher intelligence and general knowledge than those who don't read. Keeping the individual sharp as they age. Reading also relieves stress. Occasionally, when I'm reading a book, my mind may shift gears where I might have had a stressful day. These are the times when I appreciate my fictional books the most! Distracting me. Refining analytical thinking. Increasing vocabulary and writing skills.

Disabled people are treated like aliens all the time. People just don't see through the disability itself they only see the brainless, dopey one. The people who are just meant to sit there in total silence. We do have the brain power as any other normal person. A right to a say. Therefore, I hope people do read and embrace my story, because it's a general fact about the disabled and not just about me.

I still don't get it. How a person can be so confident about their disability. Broadcasting it literally, everywhere, as though it's something to be proud of. Presumably normal! Not a care in the world about people's views on it. Like my two friends, Anastasia Williams and Jam Jar. They're so open about their conditions that they're wanting and willing to talk about it with friends, on social media sites and even uploading video's regarding their disabilities on Instagram. Even, revealing their personal deformities, regardless of what people think of them. Being open is one thing. I can just about digest that but broadcasting it on social media sites is just a step too far.

There's many people out there who are outspoken about their disabilities. That's fine. But doesn't mean you have to reveal pictures and videos and plastering them all over social media sites.

I think that's just a step too far. Probably not being all there or probably they find it as a comfort for themselves. The only way to move forward and get contentment, response and sympathy.

I haven't really learned to accept my disability. But to some extent, I have gathered up the courage to say, *yeah, this is me,* to certain people and to discuss my condition with them. Telling people what they want to know, regardless of the fact I have self-confidence issues. I'm always, conscience about the people around me and what thoughts they have about me. So talking to someone about my condition is far as it goes and I would never have the confidence to post pictures, information, and talk openly about my disability on social media sites where it's open for the whole world to see; I don't think I'd want to either. I'm not that proud!

I see people saying to me, *"but at least you haven't got this or that."* Ok, I have overcome the early stages but it's all about the side effects I'm left with now, and the worsening of it. (Cerebellum Shrinkage) but the one that gets to me, is when my nerves play up and eventually bones in my body slowly and gradually deteriorate, vanish and die. Being in pain, discomfort, and agony. Currently, being my hands the first. I feel a tingling sensation where my hands close up. Being left-sided week, I have currently lost all my touch senses. An excruciating pain sliced down the side of my brain. Extremely bad headaches. Brain fog. A mist around every thought, memory, or any piece of information. I try to retrieve in my head. Sitting there long enough may bring it back, but the times it doesn't, my mind goes blank. My short-term memory is pretty bad. Storing a piece of information and literally five seconds later it's gone. Zilch. I remember, 0% of it.

Processing of information and the, inability of thought process was never all there. A tired, sleepy, feeling in my thought process. Just kind of slower thinking. A slight confusion in words and thought recollection. Unable to think and respond to anything quickly, where ordinary activities are like trying to walk through molasses. I look at something, and it takes me forever to figure out what they are. Sleep deprivation can bring it on.

I take life as it comes. Welcoming whatever, it throws at me with open arms. Life is full of obstacles, some up's and others down's. I have defiantly come far off from where I was, to think I was nothing. An immobile dead weight to now.

But remember, enjoy what you have, where you are, who you are and appreciate what you are because there will always be someone worse off than you. When life gives me every reason to be negative, I think of all the reasons to be positive, after all, there is always someone who has it worse. And, not to mention... the ones who have it better.

I've seen better days, but I've also, seen worse days. I don't have anything that I want. The many things people dream about and eventually get without even trying but, I do have all I need. I wake up with aches and pains. My life may not be perfect but I am surly blessed!

Ungrateful isn't the word! I look at people who are worse than me and just be thankful for everything I have. My sight, the ability to walk, even though it is a struggle. My voice, which to think I actually lost my speech at one point is just appalling. And the element that stands out from the rest is the fact that I'm still actually here.

OK, my future plans have gone straight through the drain pipe, but the fact is I'm still breathing and kicking, brighter than ever when my life could've gone in that flash of a moment. But no matter how hard life can get, I still try to be thankful. Hard as it is.

About the author

Me... I was born and studied in Birmingham, United Kingdom. I live with my parents, well they have split up now, but I see them both during the day. I live with dad and his mum, but occasionally I spend the night at mothers. I have four siblings including myself, however, being the one in the middle is tough. Blamed and shouted at left right and centre.

Like many people, I went to school and then on to college, but then my mid-life crises kicked in. This element of me preventing me from achieving. After a while of finding my feet again, I settled on writing as I wanted to elaborate and materialise on my original version of my biography I wrote for my English language classes in 2010. Being told that I have a writer's dream! Ever since I was told I could no longer pursue in what I was doing, I was no longer seen as having the same level as intelligence as others in my family.

I hope to inspire people with my story and I'm quite confident that after my readers have a taste of my book. I will in fact stimulate, inspire, encourage, and motivate my readers with the courage and drive never to give up! Especially for the people, who have been through a similar journey as mine. Make an impact or a difference to their lives.

Life is full of obstacles. A Stumbling block. Some ups, and some downs!

The obstruction that interferers. A barrier. Some, you can do something about and others, you can't where, it's usually out of your hand. So, before you judge me, step into my shoes and walk the life I'm living and if you get as far as I am, just maybe you will see how strong I really am!

Connect to N.A. Khan to find out more.
Fan page: https//www.facebook.com/N-Khan
Twitter: @Khan1902N

A condition that forever changed my life

A True Story
By N.A. Khan

A broken girl

A troubled past that changed her,

Physically and Mentally.

Printed in Poland
by Amazon Fulfillment
Poland Sp. z o.o., Wrocław